MIND SCIENCES

Zondervan
Guide to Cults &
Religious Movements

First Series

Second Series

MIND SCIENCES

TODD EHRENBORG
Author

Alan W. Gomes
Series Editor

ZondervanPublishingHouse
Grand Rapids, Michigan

A Division of HarperCollins*Publishers*

Mind Sciences
Copyright © 1995 by Todd Ehrenborg

Requests for information should be addressed to:
    Zondervan Publishing House
    Grand Rapids, Michigan 49530

Library of Congress Cataloging-in-Publication Data

Ehrenborg, Todd, 1950–
    Mind sciences / Todd Ehrenborg.
        p.   cm. — (Zondervan guide to cults & religious movements)
    Includes bibliographical references (p.   ).
    ISBN 0-310-48861-3 (softcover)
    1. Christian Science—controversial literature.   2. Religous Science—
    Controversial literature.   3. Unity School of Christianity—Controversial
    literature.   4. Witness bearing (Christianity)   I. Title.
    II. Series: Zondervan guide to cults and religious movements.
    BX6955.E47   1995
    289.5–dc20
                                                                                95-2140
                                                                                    CIP

Edited by James E. Ruark
Interior design by Art Jacobs

Printed in the United States of America

95 96 97 98 99 00 / ❖ DP / 10 9 8 7 6 5 4 3 2 1

# Contents

How to Use This Book

The *Zondervan Guide to Cults and Religious Movements* comprises sixteen volumes, treating many of the most important groups and belief systems confronting the Christian church today. This series distills the most important facts about each and presents a well-reasoned, cogent Christian response. The authors in this series are highly qualified, well-respected professional Christian apologists with considerable expertise on their topics.

For ease of use we have sought to maintain the same "look and feel" for all the books. We designed the structure and layout to help you find the information you need as quickly as possible.

All the volumes are written in outline form. This allows us to pack substantial content into a short book. The major divisions are basically the same from book to book. Each book contains an introduction to the cult, movement, or belief system. The introduction gives a brief history of the group, its organizational structure, and vital statistics such as membership. The theology section is arranged by doctrinal topic, such as God, Christ, sin, and salvation. The movement's position on each topic is set forth objectively, primarily from its own official writings. The group's teachings are then refuted point by point, followed by an affirmative presentation of what the Bible says about the doctrine. Following the theology section is a discussion of witnessing tips. While each witnessing encounter must be handled individually and sensitively, this section provides some helpful general guidelines, including both dos and don'ts. The books also have an annotated bibliography, listing works by the groups themselves as well as books written by Christians in response. Each book concludes with a parallel comparison chart. Arranged topically, the chart juxtaposes direct quotations from the cultic literature in the left column with the biblical refutation on the right.

One potential problem with a detailed outline is that it is easy to lose one's place in the overall structure. To overcome this problem we have provided graphical "signposts" at the top of the odd-numbered pages. Functioning like a "you are here" map in a shopping mall, these graphics show your place in the outline, including the sections that come before and after your current position. In the theology section we have also used "icons" in the margins to make clear at a glance whether the material is being presented from the cultic or Christian viewpoint. For example, in the Mormonism volume those portions of the outline presenting the Mormon position are indicated with a picture of the angel Moroni in the margin. The biblical view is shown by a drawing of a Bible.

We hope you will find these books useful as you seek "to give an answer to everyone who asks you to give the reason for the hope that you have" (1 Peter 3:15).

—Alan W. Gomes, Ph.D.
Series Editor

 # Section 1:
Christian Science

Part I: Introduction

I. Historical Background

A. *Mary Ann Morse Baker Glover Patterson Eddy (1821–1910)*

1. Mary Baker, the "Discoverer and Founder" of Christian Science (CS), was born on a farm in Bow, New Hampshire.

2. She was raised a strict Congregationalist by her parents, Mark and Abigail Baker.

3. As a child, Mary endured much physical and emotional illness, including a nervous condition that left her a semi-invalid for years. She was also afflicted with spasmodic seizures and hysterical outbursts.[1]

4. At age 17 she joined the Congregational Church at Tilton, N.H. Although she rejected their "morbid" theology (especially their teaching of double predestination[2]), she was accepted into membership.

5. Mary Ann Morse Baker married three times:

   a. In December 1843 to George W. Glover, who died seven months later of yellow fever,

   b. In June 1853 to Daniel M. Patterson, a dentist, whom she divorced for desertion,

   c. In January 1877 to Asa G. Eddy, a sewing machine salesman, who died in 1882 from a chronic heart condition. Contrary to the facts, Eddy declared that he died of "arsenic poisoning, mentally administered" by her enemies.

B. *P. P. Quimby (1802–1866) and the "Discovery" of the Mind Sciences*

1. P. P. Quimby, the Real Father of the Mind Sciences

   a. Mary Baker Eddy lived in an era when there was growing interest

---

[1]Georgine Milmine, *The Life of Mary Baker G. Eddy and the History of Christian Science* (1909; reprint, Grand Rapids: Baker, 1937), 3–25; Walter R. Martin and Norman Klann, *The Christian Science Myth* (Grand Rapids: Zondervan, 1955), 18–19.

[2]Double predestination is the teaching that God predestines certain people to damnation and others to salvation.

in transcendentalism, mesmerism,[3] metaphysics,[4] spiritualism, and mental healing.

b. Phineas Parkhurst Quimby was a metaphysical healer, who practiced mesmerism and mental healing and believed that sin, sickness, and disease exist only in the mind.

c. Quimby taught and wrote about his "Spiritual Science Healing Disease" and created a following.

d. He called his metaphysical system of healing "Science of the Christ," termed his ideas "Science of Health," and called it "Christian Science" in February 1863.[5]

2. Eddy's "Healing" by Quimby

a. During an illness in 1862, Eddy went to Portland, Maine, to seek Quimby's treatment for a "spinal inflammation."

b. Under Quimby's care she claimed to have been cured and became his committed disciple.

c. Eddy began to teach Quimby's system to others before his death.

C. *Establishing the Church*

1. Eddy's Plagiarism of Quimby

a. Eddy claimed to have discovered the principles of CS after experiencing a miraculous metaphysical healing three days after a fall on icy pavement.

(1) This discovery took place only one month after Quimby died in January 1866.

(2) Eddy claimed that the fall put her in critical condition with only three days to live.

(3) Based on her alleged healing, Eddy claimed to have "discovered" the spiritual truths of CS and devoted her life to teaching them to others.

(4) Dr. Alvin M. Cushing, the physician who treated Eddy for her fall, claimed that she was not in critical condition or near

---

[3]Franz Mesmer (1734–1815) was an Austrian physician who pioneered the practice of hypnotism. He developed a theory called "animal magnetism," later called "mesmerism." Mesmer believed all bodies contain a mysterious fluid that allows one person to have a powerful "magnetic" effect over someone else. Mrs. Eddy was fond of using the term "animal magnetism" in later years to describe all kinds of "nonexistent" evil.

[4]It is important to distinguish between metaphysics generally—which is a legitimate branch of academic philosophy—and the mind science version of it. Metaphysics is the branch of philosophy that deals with first principles and seeks to explain the nature of being or reality beyond the physical realm. Metaphysics per se is not inherently cultic or anti-Christian. Indeed, the Christian faith addresses many issues that transcend the physical realm, such as the existence of the soul. In the mind sciences, however, "metaphysics" has a different connotation, referring to a particular worldview. The characteristics of the mind science worldview are discussed throughout this book.

[5]Quimby manuscripts, 1921 edition, p. 389.

death, as she maintained. He knew of no miraculous recovery taking place in three days.

b. Eddy published *Science and Health with Key to the Scriptures* in 1875.

   (1) Eddy recorded what she had learned from Quimby and others, and used his ideas and terminology as her own. She published her new "revelation" and called it *Science and Health with Key to the Scriptures.*

   (2) Since Eddy's education was limited, she hired the Rev. J. H. Wiggin, a retired Unitarian minister, as "literary advisor" of her works from 1885 to 1891.

   (3) Eddy later denied borrowing from Quimby, but her obvious plagiarism of Quimby and others is well-documented in the *New York Times* (July 10, 1904), and *The Kingdom of the Cults,* by Dr. Walter Martin.[6]

   (4) There is testimony and evidence to show "the *very* copy of P. P. Quimby's *Manuscripts* from which Mrs. Eddy taught during the years 1867–1870, which copy also contains corrections in Mrs. Eddy's *own* handwriting."[7]

2. The Massachusetts Metaphysical College (1881–1889)

   a. At age 61 Eddy established the Massachusetts Metaphysical College in her home and allegedly taught some 4000 students at $300 each over the eight-year period.

   b. These small classes of from two to five students consisted of twelve lessons in mental healing.[8]

3. "The Church of Christ, Scientist"

   a. On August 23, 1879, Eddy founded "The Church of Christ, Scientist" to "commemorate the word and works of our Master, which should *reinstate primitive Christianity* and its *lost* element of healing."[9]

   b. In 1882, Eddy, "Mother," had fewer than fifty people who could be called followers, but only fourteen years later had well over four hundred churches and societies.

   c. Her church continued to grow to approximately one million members by the time of her death in 1910.

---

[6]Walter R. Martin, *Kingdom of the Cults* (Minneapolis: Bethany House, 1985), 128–33.
[7]Ibid., 134–35.
[8]Milmine, *The Life of Mary Baker G. Eddy,* 281–83.
[9]Christian Science *Church Manual,* 17 (emphasis added).

II. Vital Statistics

A. Membership Figures

1. The Difficulty of Assessing Precise Figures

   The totals are suppressed by CS leadership owing to the bylaws published by Eddy that prohibit publishing membership statistics.

2. Past Figures

   a. A 1936 census revealed 268,915 members in the USA.[10]

   b. In January, 1955, there were 11,000 practitioners,[11] about one million members, 3,103 branches, and 2,323 churches and societies.[12]

   c. One outside estimate placed the membership in the mid-1960s at 400,000.[13]

   d. In 1982 the Mother Church[14] admitted an annual membership loss of 1–2%, and said that almost two hundred branch churches worldwide had shut down in the previous decade.[15]

   e. The *CS Journal* listing of practitioners over the last 30 years implies a more serious decline in their numbers, from more than 11,000 worldwide in the early 1950s to about 6000 in 1978. The same trend held in California, where there were 2,200 practitioners in 1946 and only 950 in 1978 (more than in any other state).[16]

3. Present Figures

   a. Today there are 2,600 branch churches in 66 countries worldwide, plus 270 smaller groups holding services in about 20 other countries.[17]

   b. The best estimate is between 180,000 and 250,000 members worldwide.[18]

B. Crises, Controversies, and Decline

1. Controversies Involving Loss of Wealth and Influence

---

[10]*New York Times,* 12 August 1982.

[11]A "practitioner" is a devout Christian Scientist who attempts to metaphysically heal those from the "illusion" of a critical illness. The practitioner reads *Science and Health* to the client and uses the CS form of "prayer" (affirming CS truth and denying sickness or error). The faithful Christian Scientist, when experiencing the "error" of illness, is to call upon the practitioner rather than a physician.

[12]Martin and Klann, *The Christian Science Myth,* 29.

[13]*Time Magazine,* 16 June 1975, 70.

[14]The term "Mother Church" refers to the church connected with the CS headquarters in Boston.

[15]*New York Times,* 12 August 1982.

[16]*Los Angeles Times,* 16 January 1978, part 2, p. 4.

[17]*Christian Science Journal* (September 1992): 26–27.

[18]*Christian Research Journal* (Spring/Summer 1994): 42.

a. Despite its present wealth and influence, the church and the *CS Monitor* in the last three decades have shown serious losses in membership and revenue.

b. The *Christian Science Monitor* newspaper lost $138 million from 1984 to 1991.[19]

c. *Time* magazine, 27 April 1992, stated a financial loss of $235 million to the CS television Monitor Channel.

d. In 1993 the church was forced to sell off or close parts of its "troubled electronic media network" and "used $113 million of its unrestricted reserve fund and borrowed $115 million from its pension fund to finance the media empire."[20]

e. From 1987 to 1991 the available church funds dropped from $208 million to $117 million and operating expenses more than doubled from $54 million to $115 million.[21]

2. Controversies Involving Mismanagement of Funds

a. A major internal controversy occurred in 1976, when significant leaders of the Mother Church were accused by longtime members of "gross mismanagement, inexperience and lack of Christian ethics."

(1) One high-ranking CS consultant on security at the Boston headquarters, Reginald G. Kerry, 62, uncovered serious signs of decline and reported the worldwide membership of CS at about 195,000.

(2) Kerry also claimed that the number of CS practitioners was less than half of what it was in 1956, that 500 churches and societies had closed since 1972, and that 500 of the 3000 that remain were near closure.[22]

(3) The Mother Church admitted that financial reserves had been "seriously depleted" in order to build the $75 million Boston church center.[23]

(4) Kerry accused the leadership of "an alleged lack of financial accountability and alleged instances of lesbianism among the top echelon." He and others, such as actor-comedian Alan Young, a national CS lecturer and administrator, resigned and "forcefully criticized the church leadership in interviews."[24]

---

[19]*Christian Science Journal* (September 1992): 12.

[20]*Encyclopedia Britannica*, 1993 Book of the Year (Chicago: Encyclopedia Britannica, 1993), 263.

[21]*Philadelphia Inquirer*, 14 October 1991.

[22]*Time Magazine*, 15 March 1976, 44.

[23]*Time Magazine*, 15 March 1976, 44.

[24]*Los Angeles Times*, 16 January 1878, part 2, p. 4.

    b. In January 1994, a group of Christian Scientists filed suit accusing church leaders of "mismanaging funds and leaving the church $83 million in debt after a failed $450 million media venture."[25]

3. Controversies Involving Child Neglect

In the 1990s there were several court cases involving parents who failed to provide needed medical attention to sick children, choosing instead to rely on CS prayer alone.

    a. At least 18 CS children died preventable deaths since 1980 as a result of parents' not seeking professional medical treatment for children.

    b. Several CS couples were tried and convicted in court for child endangerment, and some for manslaughter. The parents had faithfully followed the CS teaching of not looking to "materia medica" (material medicine) for assistance.[26]

    c. Courts in Massachusetts repealed a law that held that spiritual healing alone is not a form of child neglect.[27]

    d. An 11-year-old Minnesota boy died of juvenile diabetes after his Christian Science mother withheld medical treatment and relied only on CS prayer. The court awarded the woman's former husband $14.2 million because of her and her new husband's negligence.[28]

    e. A similar case was filed in California by a woman against her former husband for allegedly allowing their 12-year-old diabetic son to die when he chose to treat him by CS prayer alone.[29]

4. Controversy Involving Bliss Knapp's *Destiny of the Mother Church*

    a. In 1991 and 1992 the Mother Church (headquarters in Boston) agreed to publish Bliss Knapp's controversial book, *The Destiny of the Mother Church*, written in 1947 .[30]

    b. Some considered this book blasphemous because it gives Eddy the same status as Christ.[31] Ironically, Eddy did not hesitate to declare herself equal to and the successor of Jesus Christ.[32]

    c. *The Encyclopedia Britannica* 1992 Book of the Year reported, "Subsequently, the Knapps left some $90 million to the church on

---

[25]*Christian Research Journal* (Spring/Summer 1994): 42.

[26]*The Oregonian,* 7 August 1990, A2. For documentation and many examples, see Dr. Rita Swans's *Cry of the Beloved,* available from C.H.I.L.D. Inc., Box 2604, Sioux City, IA 51106. Six such cases are discussed in the *Christian Research Journal* (Winter/Spring 1989): 5.

[27]*Christian Research Journal* (Spring/Summer 1994): 42.

[28]Ibid.

[29]Ibid.

[30]Bliss Knapp was a CS lecturer who died in 1958.

[31]*Philadelphia Inquirer,* 14 October 1991.

[32]See, for example, Eddy's *Christ and Christmas* (1907), or *Mrs. Eddy's Place* (1943).

condition that the book be published and prominently displayed in Christian Science reading rooms. Opponents of publication accused the church of condoning heresy in order to fund the controversial expansion of its media enterprises."[33]

d. To inherit the much-needed money and minimize division, the church made an obscure distinction between "authorized literature" and "Christian Science literature," claiming that "the only correct statement of Christian Science theology is found solely in the writings of our Leader, Mary Baker Eddy." This enabled them to categorize the *Destiny* book with other historical works or "reminiscences" published or sold by the CS Publishing Society and yet not considered official "Christian Science literature." In protest many members and officials have resigned since May 1993, and some groups have broken away from the church.[34]

e. Although the Mother Church printed and distributed the book, she was unable to claim the full amount of the money in the courts and was forced to share nearly half of it with Stanford University and the Los Angeles County Art Museum.[35]

C. Literature Distribution

1. Books

   Science and Health with Key to the Scriptures (published in seventeen languages) and sixteen other books written by Eddy are distributed worldwide through some 2,500 CS Reading Rooms, college campus organizations, local churches, and outreach by CS radio and television.

2. Newspaper and Magazines

   a. *The Christian Science Monitor* (international daily newspaper in 147 countries)

   b. *Christian Science Quarterly Bible Lessons* (uniform lessons used worldwide for daily study of the Bible and *Science and Health*) in 14 languages

   c. *Christian Science Journal* (monthly; includes worldwide directory of churches, practitioners, nurses, and teachers)

   d. The *Christian Science Sentinel* (weekly testimonials)

   e. *The Herald of Christian Science* (monthly articles and testimonials)

   f. *World Monitor* (monthly international news magazine)

3. Television and Radio

   a. CS leadership decided in 1992 to discontinue television broadcasting in an estimated shutdown cost of $68.5 million. All regular

---

[33]*Encyclopedia Britannica,* 1992 Book of the Year, "Religion" (Chicago: Encyclopedia Britannica, 1992), 262.

[34]*Christian Science Journal* (September 1992): 20–21.

[35]*Christian Research Journal* (Winter 1992): 6, 35.

television programming was canceled by late 1994.

    (1) The Herald of Christian Science (radio; television programming canceled)

    (2) World Monitor Television (canceled in 1992)

    (3) MonitoRadio (radio news service of the CS Monitor)

    (4) Worldservice of the CS Monitor (short-wave radio)

    (5) WQTV Television, Channel 68, Boston (purchased in November 1993 by WABU-TV, Boston University Communications, Inc.)

  b. Funds from the Bliss Knapp estate may salvage some media enterprises in the future.[36]

4. Church Services

  a. The CS church conducts Sunday worship and Sunday schools; the two "pastors" of the church are *Science and Health* and the Bible, which are both read during services in the place of sermons.

  b. Wednesday evening testimonial meetings take place, in which Christian Scientists give thanks for Mary Baker Eddy and for their healing through metaphysics.[37]

  c. University and college organizations provide services and outreach to students.

  d. CS Reading Rooms are sometimes used for services when the congregation is small.

  e. The Board of Lectureship sends lecturers throughout the world to speak on CS.

D. Related Groups

Various metaphysical groups that admire Eddy but do not follow her exclusively are United Christian Scientists; International Metaphysical Association; Margaret Laird Foundation; The Infinite Way; and the Plainfield (N. J.) C. S. Church.

---

[36] *Christian Science Journal* (September 1992): 13.

[37] For examples see *One Hundred Years of Christian Science Healing* (Boston: CS Publishing Society, 1966).

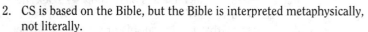

Part II: Theology

I. The Doctrine of Revelation and Scripture

A. *The Christian Science Position on Revelation and Scripture Briefly Stated*

1. To properly understand the Bible one needs Eddy's higher, final revelation, *Science and Health with Key to the Scriptures,* which correctly interprets "true Christianity."

2. CS is based on the Bible, but the Bible is interpreted metaphysically, not literally.

3. Jesus was a master metaphysician who taught these Truths of Divine metaphysics.

B. *Arguments Used by Christian Scientists to Support Their Position on Revelation and Scripture*

1. To properly understand the true, spiritual interpretation of the Bible one needs Eddy's higher, final revelation.

   a. *Science and Health with Key to the Scriptures* is the voice of Truth to this age, our final authority, and is needed to understand the Bible accurately.[38]

   b. *Science and Health* unlocks the mysteries of the Bible so we can understand their truer, spiritual, metaphysical meanings.[39]

   (1) These higher meanings must be substituted for the normal English, or "material," definitions to understand their original inspired meanings.[40]

   (2) For example, we know that the *Holy Spirit* is Divine Science because God revealed it to Eddy, God's chosen revelator of Christ, Truth, in this age.[41]

   c. CS is the final and only authority for understanding the absolute Divine Principle. It completes what Jesus only began.[42]

   d. The Bible is unreliable and contains many falsehoods.[43] Therefore we cannot depend on it by itself.

---

[38] Mary Baker Eddy, *Science and Health with Key to the Scriptures,* 1971 ed., 107, 456–57 (hereafter abbreviated as *S/H*).

[39] *S/H,* 99.

[40] *S/H,* 579.

[41] *Mrs. Eddy's Place* (Boston: CS Publishing Society, 1943).

[42] *S/H,* 107, 147.

[43] *S/H,* 139, 521, 524, 545.

   (1) The Bible must be interpreted by Eddy's *Science and Health with Key to the Scriptures* rather than judging *Science and Health* by the Bible.[44]

   (2) The revelation given to Eddy was from God and is "higher, clearer, and more permanent" than any given in the Bible. Christian Science is unerring and Divine.[45]

  e. All other religious systems are therefore inferior and built on shaky foundations.[46]

 2. CS is based on the Bible, but the Bible is interpreted metaphysically, not literally.

  a. In discovering CS, the Bible was Eddy's only textbook and only authority.[47] God revealed to her the "inspired" Word of the Bible, demonstrating that the literal, historical record of the Bible is unimportant in knowing God.[48]

  b. The Bible is full of metaphors and names that must be spiritually interpreted. A spiritual understanding is a metaphysical understanding, not a literal one, for God is Spirit and must be understood spiritually.

  c. There is a dual meaning to every Bible passage. The literal, or material, reading of the text is the reading of the carnal mind, which is enmity toward God (Rom. 8:7). The one important interpretation of the Bible is the spiritual (metaphysical) one.[49]

  d. The many mistakes in the Bible and its many ancient versions show how the literal, historical interpretation of the Bible is useless and often the source of unbelief and hopelessness.[50]

  e. Jesus' method of interpretation was strictly metaphysical.[51]

 3. Jesus was a master metaphysician who taught these Truths of Divine metaphysics.

  a. Jesus of Nazareth was the most "scientific" or metaphysical man in history.[52] He was the true demonstrator of Divine Science and our example.[53]

---

[44]*S/H*, 579.

[45]*S/H*, 99; *Mrs. Eddy's Place.*

[46]*S/H*, 269.

[47]*S/H*, 110, 126, 479.

[48]*S/H*, 146; Mary Baker Eddy, *Miscellaneous Writings,* 1896 ed. (Boston: CS Publishing Society), 169–70 (hereafter cited as *Misc. Writ.*); *S/H*, 537.

[49]*Misc. Writ.*, 169; *S/H*, 319–20.

[50]*Misc. Writ.*, 169.

[51]*Misc. Writ.*, 170.

[52]*S/H*, 313.

[53]*S/H*, 329, 18.

b. He healed the sick and taught the divine Principle to his students, but left no definite rule for demonstrating this Principle of healing.[54]

    c. Eddy discovered this rule and teaches it in CS, which alone reveals the divine Principle and fully demonstrates it.[55] Her work is "complementary to that of Christ Jesus" because she was chosen by God to fulfill prophecy by giving the "full and final" revelation of Truth.[56]

C. *Refutation of Arguments Used by Christian Scientists to Support Their Position on Revelation and Scripture*

  1. The Bible is complete and final. Therefore another "revelation" is not needed (see Section D).

  2. The metaphysical interpretation of the Bible is totally subjective, unverifiable, and therefore useless.

    a. Unlike the normal, literal method of interpretation, there is no objective way to prove whether a metaphysician's interpretation is right or wrong.

    b. Even a supposed healing does not prove that the CS view is correct, because the Bible claims there are *counterfeit* healing miracles as well as authentic ones (e.g., Ex. 7:11–12, 22; 8:7, 18–19; 9:11; 2 Thess. 2:8–11).

  3. Eddy wrongly divorces the spiritual from the literal meaning of Bible texts.

    a. In Scripture, Jesus and others interpreted the Old Testament in such a way that the spiritual meaning they gave was always built upon the literal meaning of the text. Nowhere does the Bible divorce the literal and spiritual meanings.

    b. Consider that Jesus uses his parables as a teaching device in their natural and normal manner, i.e., to make a comparison by analogy.

      (1) In the sower and the soils (Matt. 13:1–10), Jesus interpreted his own parable literally in verses 18–23.

      (2) In the weeds (Matt. 13:24–30), he interprets literally in verses 36–43.

  4. Jesus interpreted the Bible (i.e., the Old Testament) literally, not metaphysically (see Section D).

  5. The Bible does not contain mistakes.

    a. While only the original biblical manuscripts were completely without error, it is not true, as Eddy states, that there are thousands of errors in the texts that we have today.

---

[54]*S/H*, 147, 473.
[55]*S/H*, 147.
[56]*Mrs. Eddy's Place.*

b. The science of textual criticism has demonstrated the extremely high accuracy of both the Old and the New Testament manuscripts.[57]

D. Arguments Used to Prove the Biblical View of Revelation and Scripture

1. The Bible claims to be reliable and authoritative.

   a. The Bible is explicitly called the Word of God (Heb. 4:12; Gal. 1:11–12), perfect and trustworthy (Pss. 19:7; 119:89, 140). It is inspired by God (2 Tim. 3:16; 2 Peter 1:20–21; Matt. 5:17–18), has complete authority and reliability (John 10:35; 1 Peter 4:11), stands forever (Isa. 40:8; Matt. 24:35), is truth (John 17:17; Ps. 119:160), and is the final authority by which to judge all teaching (Isa. 8:20; 1 Thess. 5:21; Acts 17:11).

   b. Jesus affirmed its complete authority (Matt. 4:4, 7, 10; 5:17–18, 39; 12:40; 22:29–32, 43; 24:35; Luke 24:25; John 10:35; 17:17).

   c. The Bible claims that its very words are inspired (Ex. 4:12; 19:3–6; Lev. 1:1; Num. 7:89; 12:6, 8; 1 Sam. 3:4–14, 21; 9:15; Isa. 6:8–9; Rev. 14:13).

2. The Bible is complete and final.

   a. Jude 3 urges us to "contend for *the faith* that was *once for all entrusted* to the saints."

      (1) "'The faith' is the body of truth that very early in the church's history took on a definite form (cf. Acts 2:42; Rom. 6:17; Gal. 1:23)."[58]

      (2) "Once and for all" (Greek: *hapax*) means something that has been done for all time, something that never needs to be repeated or cannot be changed.

      (3) "Entrusted," in Greek, refers to an act that was completed in the past with no continuing action. This verb tense[59] means a once-and-for-all completed action. This means there is no need for Eddy's "new," additional "revelation."

   b. Other verses likewise demonstrate that no further progressive revelation beyond the Bible is needed (Ps. 119:89; Heb. 1:1–2; Luke 16:19–31).

---

[57]On the accuracy of the biblical manuscripts see Oswald T. Allis, *The Old Testament: Its Claims and Its Critics* (Nutley, N.J.: Presbyterian and Reformed, 1972); F. F. Bruce, *The New Testament Documents: Are They Reliable?* (Downers Grove, Ill.: InterVarsity Press, 1960); *The Books and the Parchments* (Old Tappan, N.J.: Revell, 1953); Josh McDowell, *Evidence That Demands a Verdict: Historical Evidence for the Christian Faith* (Arrowhead Springs, Calif.: Campus Crusade for Christ, 1972); *More Evidence That Demands a Verdict: Historical Evidences for the Christian Scriptures* (Arrowhead Springs, Calif.: Campus Crusade for Christ, 1975); *More Than a Carpenter* (Wheaton, Ill.: Tyndale, 1980).

[58]Edwin A. Blum, "Jude," in *Expositor's Bible Commentary*, vol. 12, ed. Frank E. Gaebelein (Grand Rapids: Zondervan, 1981), 388.

[59]That is, an aorist passive participle.

c. God commands that we do not add to or take away from (Deut. 4:2; 12:32; Prov. 30:6; Gal. 3:15; Rev. 22:18–19), corrupt (2 Cor. 2:17), handle deceitfully (2 Cor. 4:2), or distort (2 Peter 3:16) the Holy Scriptures. These prohibitions would certainly apply to superimposing a metaphysical interpretation over the Scriptures, which was never intended or prescribed.

3. Jesus and the New Testament writers consistently interpreted the Old Testament literally.

   a. Jesus treated the historical context as essential (Matt. 12:40; 13:13–18, 35; 24:37; Mark 10:3–9; Luke 17:26).

   b. Jesus treated all Scripture as authoritative (Matt. 4:4, 7, 10; 5:17; Luke 24:44), every word as essential (Luke 16:17; 24:25), and all of Scripture as infallible and inspired (John 10:35; Matt. 22:43).

   c. Jesus' literal hermeneutic (method of interpretation) is evident when he interpreted scriptural events as being literal and persons as actual, such as the creation of Adam and Eve (Matt. 25:34; Mark 10:6; 13:19); the existence of Abraham, Isaac, Jacob, and Moses (Mark 12:26–27; Luke 5:14; 20:37–38; John 5:45–47; 6:32); Jonah and the huge fish (Matt. 12:39–41); Noah's ark (Matt. 24:37–39; Luke 17:26–27); Sodom, Gomorrah, and Lot (Matt. 10:15; Luke 17:28–29); Elijah and Elisha (Luke 4:24–27); Judas' predicted betrayal (Ps. 41:9 with Matt. 26:23–24, 54); and Jesus' predicted rejection (Luke 20:17–19).

   d. Jesus always described the fulfillment of his prophetic statements as literally historical rather than metaphysical (Matt. 17:9, 22–23; 20:17–19, 28; 26:31–34; Mark 10:33–34; Luke 9:22, 44; 18:31–33; 24:46–47; John 13:18–19; Acts 1:8).

II. The Doctrine of God and the Trinity

A. *The Christian Science Position on God Briefly Stated*

   1. God, Divine Mind, is impersonal yet individual.

   2. God, "It," is a triply divine Principle or Mind: Life, Truth, and Love.

   3. God is "All-in-all"; matter is illusion.

   4. Everything in the universe is a unified whole, expressed as "all is one."

   5. The Holy Spirit is Divine Science, the universal expression of CS.

B. *Arguments Used by Christian Scientists to Support Their Position on God*

   1. God, Divine Mind, is impersonal yet individual.

      a. God is not a person because Spirit, Mind, and Principle cannot be as limited as a person.

b. God is individual and yet not a person. God is Spirit and infinitely more than a person. Science defines the individuality of God as supreme good, Life, Truth, and Love.[60]

c. The best understanding of God is as divine Principle, Love, rather than personality.[61] Therefore we do not approach God in a personal way, because prayer cannot change God or his ways.[62]

d. Eddy taught, "Prayer to a personal God hinders spiritual growth" because Divine Mind is devoid of "personality."[63]

2. God, "It," is a triply divine Principle or Mind: Life, Truth, and Love.

a. The Trinity represents a Trinity of Being, not of persons.

b. Principle is impersonal, so there cannot be three eternal Divine Personalities called Father, Son, and Holy Spirit, because this suggests pagan gods rather than the one ever-present I AM.[64]

c. God is Spirit. Science (Divine metaphysics) teaches us that the true spiritual meaning of "Trinity" must refer to a triply divine Principle: Life, Truth, and Love. They represent a trinity in unity, three in one, the same in essence though with differing offices. These three are called God the Father-Mother; Christ the spiritual idea of sonship; and divine Science or the Holy Comforter. They express the three-part nature of the infinite and the divine Principle of scientific being.[65]

d. The Holy Spirit cannot be a person because God is impersonal.

(1) Eddy's revelation states that the Holy Spirit, Holy Ghost, or Comforter, is Divine Science, the development of eternal Life, Truth, and Love.[66] The Holy Spirit cannot be a third person of a Trinity, because God is impersonal and one.

(2) The Holy Spirit reveals the divine Principle, Love, and leads us into all truth as Jesus promised.[67] Divine Science is the universal expression of Christian Science, and this Science is what Jesus demonstrated in his life and ministry.[68]

---

[60]R.D.S., 1–2. R.D.S. = *Rudimental Divine Science* by Mary Baker Eddy, 1909 ed. (Boston: CS Publishing Society).

[61]*S/H*, 473.

[62]*No and Yes*, 39–40.

[63]Quoted in I. M. Haldeman, *Christian Science in the Light of Holy Scriptures*, (n.p.: n.d.) 268. While emphasizing God as Impersonal (473:23–25), once or twice Eddy seems to hint that God somehow has a personal element to his make-up (*S/H*, 116:24–30). Later, she seems to back away from that by being willing to admit only that God is personal in merely a scientific sense (*S/H*, 336–37). In other words, to Eddy, God is personal only in the sense that metaphysically he is reflected in the spiritual idea, which is mankind.

[64]*S/H*, 256, 331–32.

[65]*S/H*, 331–32.

[66]*S/H*, 588:7–8; 55:27–29.

[67]*S/H*, 332:2–22.

[68]*S/H*, 43.

      (3) The coming of the Holy Spirit on Pentecost, for example, was an influx of the universal truths of Divine Science.[69]

3. God is "All-in-all"; matter is illusion.

    a. Because God is All, everything must be God.

    b. God is All-in-all; God is Infinite Mind, Soul, Spirit, Life, Truth, Love, intelligence; all matter is mortal error and has no real existence.[70] Nothing possesses reality or existence except Divine Mind and its ideas.[71]

    c. "There is no life, truth, intelligence, nor substance in matter. All is infinite Mind and its infinite manifestation, for God is All-in-all. Spirit is immortal Truth; matter is mortal error. Spirit is the real and eternal; matter is the unreal and temporal. Spirit is God, and man is His image and likeness. Therefore, man is not material; he is spiritual."[72]

    d. God is the only true reality and everything else is illusion.

    e. Whatever is good is God, and whatever is not God does not really exist. Since God is perfectly good, Divine Mind can therefore have nothing to do with the wrathful Jehovah God of the Bible.[73]

4. The Bible supports the Christian Science view of God.

    a. Verses such as 1 John 4:8, 16; Matthew 5:25–26; 6:22–23; Mark 5:39; John 8:44; Romans 8:2, 31; and James 1:13 support the CS view.

    b. Consider 1 John 4:8, "God is love." Eddy likewise stated:

      (1) "The real Christian Scientist is constantly accentuating harmony in word and deed, mentally and orally, perpetually repeating this diapason of heaven: 'Good is my God, and my God is Good. Love is my God, and my God is Love.'"[74]

      (2) "It is logical that because God is Love, Love is divine Principle; then Love as either divine Principle or Person stands for God—or both have the nature of God."[75]

C. Refutation of Arguments Used by Christian Scientists to Support Their Position on God

1. Contrary to Eddy, the God of the Bible is a personal being, not an impersonal Principle or "It."

---

[69]*S/H*, 43:7–10.

[70]*S/H*, 113, 116, 425, 503.

[71]*S/H*, 331.

[72]*S/H*, 468:9ff. Eddy calls this "the scientific statement of being."

[73]*S/H*, 524.

[74]*Misc. Writ.*, 206.

[75]"Message to the Mother Church," (June 1901), 3, vv. 21–28.

2. The God of the Bible is a triune being.

   Throughout the Bible God reveals himself as a triune personal God; as three eternal, distinct persons manifesting themselves as Father, Son, and Holy Spirit, all with one-and-the-same divine nature.

3. The Bible teaches that the Holy Spirit is the third person of the Holy Trinity.

   a. Eddy has no biblical basis to teach that the Holy Spirit is "Divine Science." This was a deceptive metaphysical catchphrase popular in her day, which she probably borrowed from P. P. Quimby or another metaphysical teacher.

   b. Jesus himself described the Holy Spirit in John 14–16 very differently from Eddy. He described the third person of the Trinity in terms of a personality, never in terms of an impersonal force.

4. Pantheism is false.

   a. There is a contradiction in the view that we *come to realize* our divinity through CS. If God is absolute, unchanging reality (as CS affirms), how can we be a part of God and yet change from ignorance of our divinity to a realization of it? If we do, we cannot be God, since God cannot change. If we *become* God, or a part of God, then we and God have changed, making us both changeable beings and not immutable.[76]

   b. The totality of things includes evil (Ex. 4:11; Prov. 16:4; Isa. 45:7; 54:16; Jer. 4:6), but God is not evil (Matt. 5:48). If everything is God, then God must include evil, which is clearly false.

5. The Bible does not teach monism (all is one).

   a. Monism is the belief that all of reality is one, a unified whole. Hinduism, not Christianity, is based on this idea that all is divine.

   b. The God of the Bible has revealed himself as a personal being who is separate in nature from, yet involved in, his creation.

   c. The verses Christian Scientists use to prove monism are taken out of context (see above, Point II.B.4.).

   For example, the biblical statement "God is love" (1 John 4:8) means that God is by nature love; love is essential to who and what he is. However, it is not true that "Love is God." For the CS statement to be true, the Scriptures would have to teach "love is God," which they do not.[77]

---

[76]Norman Geisler and Ron Brooks, *When Skeptics Ask: A Handbook on Christian Evidences* (Wheaton: Ill.: Victor Books, 1990), 46.

[77]In the Greek of 1 John 4:8 the placement of the definite article (*the*) keeps us from translating the text as "love is God"; this passage can only be translated as "God is love." Biblical scholar A. T. Robertson observes the placement of the definite article and notes, "John does not say that love is God, but only that God is love. The two terms are not interchangeable" (*Word Pictures in the New Testament* [Nashville: Broadman, 1933], 6:232).

6. The Bible contradicts the dualistic view of Christian Science.

   a. The dualism that CS (and other mind scientists) believe exists between the goodness of spirit and the evil of matter comes from Neoplatonic and Gnostic thought rather than the Bible.[78]

   b. The Bible teaches that God is Spirit and created all matter (Gen. 1:1–31), and he "saw all that he had made and it was very *good*" (v. 31). While the Bible teaches a difference in nature between God and his creation, it never declares his created order evil or nonexistent.

   c. The Bible affirms that material things are not by nature evil, but because they possess a God-given value and goodness they are to be received with thanksgiving and dedicated to his purposes (1 Tim. 4:4). It declares "sin" as being evil, not the body or the flesh (Rom. 7:17).

7. The Christian Science denial of matter is absurd.

   a. To simply deny the existence of matter and affirm only "Spirit," as Eddy does, is a metaphysical manipulation that flies in the face of everyday experience and reason. Simply denying the existence of matter (or sin, sickness, and death) does not automatically negate its reality.

   b. Ask the Christian Scientist, "If all matter is a false illusion, where did *the idea* of its existence come from?"

   c. We vividly experience the material world, so it must have a source, and therefore something real exists besides God. Why is this "illusion" so strong that all people, including Christian Scientists, go to the dentist, have sexual relations to produce children, or eat in order to stay healthy? If matter does not exist, why would Eddy recommend a hypodermic injection for the relief of severe pain?[79]

D. Arguments Used to Prove the Biblical Doctrine of God

1. The God of the Bible is personal.

   a. God is personal and manifests a subject-object relationship with his Son Jesus Christ (Matt. 3:17; Mark 1:11; Luke 3:22; John 16:32; 17:1–3) and with us (Ex. 3:14; 33:11–23; Rev. 3:20). He seeks a personal relationship with us and commands us to seek him (Isa. 55:6) and pray to him (Jer. 33:3). He promises that he will respond according to our particular need (2 Chron. 7:12–14).

---

[78]Gnosticism (Greek: *gnosis*, knowledge) is a collective name for a diverse number of pantheistic sects that taught "salvation by knowledge." The Gnostics claimed a superior spiritual knowledge that even the apostles of Jesus did not possess. See Samuel Macauley Jackson, ed. in chief, *The Schaff-Herzog Encyclopedia of Religious Knowledge* (Grand Rapids: Baker, 1977), 496–500; *Eerdmans' Handbook to the World's Religions* (Grand Rapids: Eerdmans, 1982), 110–13, 45, 379; and Merrill C. Tenney, gen. ed., *Zondervan Pictorial Encyclopedia of the Bible* (Grand Rapids: Zondervan), 2:736–39.

[79]*S/H*, 464.

     b. God manifests traits of personality: he has mind (1 Sam. 15:29; Heb. 7:21), will (Matt. 6:10), and emotions (Gen. 6:6); he remembers (Isa. 43:25), speaks (Isa. 42:8), hears (Ex. 2:24), sees (Gen. 6:5), creates (Gen. 1:1), knows (Jer. 29:11; 2 Tim. 2:19; 1 John 3:20), judges (Ezek. 18:30), and plans (Eph. 1:11).

     c. He is a personal spirit (John 4:24; Gen. 17:1; Heb. 11:6), often referred to with personal pronouns.

2. The God of the Bible is triune.

     a. Within the nature of the one God there are three eternal persons: God the Father, God the Son, and God the Holy Spirit. They have the same attributes and are the one God.

     b. While there is only one God (Deut. 6:4; Isa. 43:10; 44:6; 46:9; Mark 12:32; 1 Cor. 8:4; James 2:19), the Bible describes this Being as three in person:

        (1) The Father is called God (Phil. 2:11; 2 Peter 1:17; Rom. 15:6; 1 Cor. 8:6).

        (2) The Son is called God (John 1:1, 14, 18; 5:18; 8:58 with Ex. 3:14; John 10:30–33; 17:22; 19:7; 20:28; Rom. 9:5; Heb. 1:3, 8; Phil. 2:6–12; Col. 2:9; Titus 2:13; 1 Tim. 1:16–17; 2 Peter 1:1; Jer. 23:6; Mic. 5:2). (Additional verses on the deity of Christ are given under the section on Jesus Christ, Point III.D. below.)

        (3) The Holy Spirit is called God (Gen. 1:2; 6:3; Isa. 61:1; Acts 5:1–4; 2 Cor. 3:17; Heb. 9:14).

     c. All three persons share the same uniquely divine attributes.

        (1) Omnipotence: *Father* (Jer. 32:17); *Son* (Matt. 28:18; 1 Tim. 6:15; Col. 1:16–17; Heb. 1:3); *Holy Spirit* (Luke 1:35, 37); *God* (Matt. 19:26; Rev. 19:6).

        (2) Omniscience: *Father* (Ps. 139:1–6); *Son* (Matt. 12:25; John 2:24; 6:64; 16:30; Col. 2:3); *Holy Spirit* (Ezek. 11:5; 1 Cor. 2:10).

        (3) Omnipresence: *Father* (Jer. 23:24); *Son* (Matt. 18:20; 28:20; Gal. 2:20; Rev. 3:20); *Holy Spirit* (Ps. 139:7–10).

        (4) Eternality: *Father* (Deut. 33:27); *Son* (Mic. 5:2; Col. 1:17; Heb. 13:8); *Holy Spirit* (Heb. 9:14).

     d. All three share the same divine work.

        (1) Creation: *Father* (Isa. 64:8); *Son* (Col. 1:16; John 1:3; Heb. 1:2); *Holy Spirit* (Ps. 104:30).

        (2) Resurrection of Jesus Christ: *Father* (1 Thess. 1:10); *Son* (John 2:19); *Holy Spirit* (1 Peter 3:18); *God* (Acts 17:30–31).

        (3) Life-Giver: *Father* (John 5:21); *Son* (John 6:39); *Holy Spirit* (1 Peter 3:18).

        (4) Sanctifier: *Father* (Jude 1); *Son* (Heb. 2:11); *Holy Spirit* (1 Peter 1:2).

(5) Indweller: *Father* (John 14:23); *Son* (Eph. 3:17); *Holy Spirit* (John 14:17); *God* (2 Cor. 6:16).

(6) Coming King: *Jehovah* (Rev. 1:8; 22:6–7, 12, 20); *Son* (Matt. 24:3, 27, 30, 37; 1 Thess. 4:13–17).

3. God is separate from his creation.

a. There is a sharp biblical distinction between the nature of God and his creation (Num. 23:19; Ps. 102:25–27; Eccl. 5:2; Isa. 31:3; 40:22–26; 44:24; Rom. 1:20–25).

b. The world depends upon God for its continued existence (Acts 17:28; Col. 1:16–17), but he is not "one" with the universe (Isa. 45:18).

c. God is not all-in-all in any pantheistic sense (Eph. 4:6; Heb. 1:2, 12; 2 Peter 3:10). He created all things material and spiritual out of nothing (Gen. 1:1; Neh. 9:6; Ps. 33:9; 89:11; John 1:3; Acts 17:24; Col. 1:16–17; Heb. 3:4; 11:3; Rev. 4:11; 10:6). Creation was a free act of his will (Job 38:4–11; Ps. 33:1–9; 121:2; Zech. 12:1; Heb. 11:3).

d. God is transcendent (i.e., above and distinct from creation). He is independent and different from his creatures (Job 11:7–9; Isa. 40:12–26; 55:8–9).

e. God's immanence identifies God as active within creation, yet distinct from it in terms of his nature (Deut. 4:7; Ps. 19; 139; Hos. 11:9; Rom. 1:20).

f. The biblical view combines transcendence and immanence as compatible with each other (Isa. 57:15; Jer. 23:23–24; Ezek. 11:22–23; Acts 17:22–31).

4. The Holy Spirit is the third eternal person of the triune God.

a. He is referred to with personal pronouns (John 14:16–17; 16:7–14, etc.).

b. He is described in terms of personality: he has mind (John 15:26), will (1 Cor. 12:11), and emotions (Rom. 15:30).

c. He speaks (2 Peter 1:21), strives with the ungodly (Gen. 6:3), forbids (Acts 16:6–7), foretells (Acts 1:16), can be blasphemed (Matt. 12:31), can be grieved (Eph. 4:30), teaches (Luke 12:12), thinks and makes decisions (Acts 15:28), can be lied to (Acts 5:3), sanctifies us (Rom. 8:26–27), and took part in the creation of matter (Isa. 40:12–14).

d. He is eternal (Heb. 9:14), all-powerful (1 Cor. 12:7), all-knowing (1 Cor. 2:10), ever-present (Ps. 139:7–10), and shares the same divine nature as the Father and the Son (Matt. 3:16; 28:18; Luke 1:35; John 14:16; 2 Cor. 13:14).

e. He is called God (Isa. 6:8–10 with Acts 28:25–27; Jer. 31:31–34 with Heb. 10:15–16; John 3:6 with 1 John 5:4; Acts 5:3–4; 1 Cor. 3:16–17 with 6:19–20; Heb. 3:7–9 with Ex. 17:2–7; 2 Peter 1:20–21 with 2 Tim. 3:16).

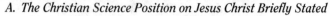

III. The Person of Jesus Christ

A. *The Christian Science Position on Jesus Christ Briefly Stated*

1. Jesus was merely a human man, a divine idea (or an idea of God). Eddy defines Jesus as "the highest human corporeal concept of the divine idea."[80]

2. Jesus was the Son of God, but not God the Son.

3. Jesus was not the Christ. "Christ = The divine manifestation of God, which comes to the flesh to destroy incarnate error."[81]

4. "Jesus = The highest human corporeal concept of the divine idea, rebuking and destroying error and bringing to light man's immortality."[82]

5. Jesus is our Way-shower to salvation, but he cannot save us.

B. *Arguments Used by Christian Scientists to Support Their Position on Jesus Christ*

1. Jesus was merely a human man who best demonstrated the Christ.

   a. He is the highest human concept of the perfect man.[83]

   b. Jesus presented the ideal of God better than any man could because of his spiritual origin.

   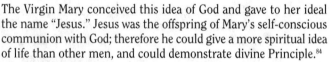

   The Virgin Mary conceived this idea of God and gave to her ideal the name "Jesus." Jesus was the offspring of Mary's self-conscious communion with God; therefore he could give a more spiritual idea of life than other men, and could demonstrate divine Principle.[84]

2. Jesus is not God, but the Son of God.

   a. Jesus is the Son of God, a divine idea, like all mortals, yet he is not God the Son, just as he declared.[85]

   b. "God is infinitely more than a person or finite form can contain." God could not enter a man, or God would be finite and become less than God. God's fullness could never be reflected by a single man, even Jesus.[86] Spirit cannot mingle with flesh, which is mere illusion.[87]

---

[80]*S/H*, 589.

[81]*S/H*, 583.

[82]*S/H*, 589.

[83]*S/H*, 482.

[84]*S/H*, 25, 29–30. In other words, CS would argue that Jesus could best demonstrate the Christ because his mother conceived him as a spiritual idea, thereby showing her great spiritual understanding of Spirit as being the only reality.

[85]*S/H*, 361.

[86]*Misc. Writ.*, 16; *S/H*, 336.

[87]*S/H*, 591:8–15.

3. Jesus was not the Christ.

   a. "Jesus is the human man, and Christ is the divine idea," which is the dualism of Jesus the Christ.[88] Jesus is not the Christ, but "the highest human corporeal concept of the divine idea."[89] He only represented and demonstrated the Christ, the true idea of God.[90]

   b. The Christ, Truth, was demonstrated through the man Jesus to prove the power of Spirit over flesh.[91] The Christ was the only divinity of the man Jesus.[92]

   c. Jesus cannot be the Christ and never claimed to be. Jesus was fallible, but the Christ is infallible.[93]

   d. Jesus came in the first century as a human and departed this earth, but the Christ, which is spiritual, is eternal.[94]

   e. In any event, the man Jesus is not really important because it makes no difference whether or not he ever lived.[95]

4. Jesus was only a Way-shower.

   a. Jesus was the Way-shower to God,[96] meaning that he was the example of how to save ourselves.[97]

   b. He did not come to do the work of salvation for us, because people must "work out their own salvation."[98]

C. *Refutation of Christian Science Arguments Used to Support Their Position on Jesus Christ*

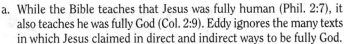

1. Jesus is fully human, but he is also fully God (see Point D).

   a. While the Bible teaches that Jesus was fully human (Phil. 2:7), it also teaches he was fully God (Col. 2:9). Eddy ignores the many texts in which Jesus claimed in direct and indirect ways to be fully God.

   b. We agree that God is infinitely more than a human form can contain. However, in the miracle of the incarnation, the eternal Word of God assumed a human nature in the person of Jesus of Nazareth. The miracle of the incarnation states that Jesus Christ was one unique person with two natures (Rom. 9:5), being fully human (Heb. 2:14–15) and fully divine (John 8:58).

---

[88]*S/H*, 473.
[89]*S/H*, 589.
[90]*S/H*, 316; 332–34; 473.
[91]*S/H*, 316.
[92]*S/H*, 26.
[93]*Misc. Writ.*, 84.
[94]*S/H*, 333–34.
[95]*Misc. Writ.*, 84.
[96]*S/H*, 30, 288, 497.
[97]*S/H*, 18.
[98]*S/H*, 22.

    c. When the Word became flesh and dwelt among us (John 1:1, 14) he did not become less than God, though he gave up the independent exercise of some divine attributes (John 14:28; Phil. 2:5–11).

2. Jesus is explicitly called "the Christ" many times.

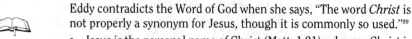

Eddy contradicts the Word of God when she says, "The word *Christ* is not properly a synonym for Jesus, though it is commonly so used."[99]

    a. Jesus is the personal name of Christ (Matt. 1:21), whereas Christ is his official name which denotes his title or office (Matt. 16:16).

       Christ is the Greek equivalent of the Hebrew word *mashiach*, meaning "the Anointed One" or "Messiah." *Messiah* and *Christ* are titles that refer to the same person, Jesus.

    b. It is a logical fallacy to believe that Jesus could not be the eternal Christ just because he was born on earth at a specific time and departed. The Bible explains that Jesus preexisted as the eternal Word of God before his birth in Bethlehem (Isa. 9:6; Mic. 5:2; John 1:1, 30; 8:58; Col. 1:17; 1 John 1:1).[100]

    c. Christ is never called a "divine idea" in the Bible.

       Jesus of Nazareth is the One anointed with the Spirit and power (Acts 10:38) to be the true Messiah or Christ (John 1:41; Rom. 9:5). There is no distinction, therefore, between Jesus and his title, Christ, or any of his other titles. God says that anyone who denies this is a deceiver and aligned with the antichrist (1 John 4:3; 2 John 7).

    d. Many people in the Bible specifically identified Jesus as the Christ.

       (1) John the Apostle wrote so that we would believe Jesus is the Christ (John 20:31).

       (2) Peter proclaimed that Jesus was the Christ and was blessed by Jesus himself for it (Matt. 16:16–20). Did Jesus lie to Peter?

       (3) Martha, who knew Jesus well, proclaimed him to be the Christ (John 11:27).

       (4) God has made Jesus both Lord and Christ (Acts 2:36).

       (5) Paul proved regularly to the Jews that Jesus was the Christ (Acts 9:22; 17:3; 18:5).

       (6) The apostles "never stopped teaching and proclaiming the good news that Jesus is the Christ" (Acts 5:42).

       (7) Apollos (who was called "mighty in the Scriptures" [Acts 18:24 KJV]) demonstrated by the Scriptures that Jesus was the Christ (Acts 18:28).

---

[99]*S/H*, 333.

[100]See Ron Rhodes, *Christ Before the Manger* (Grand Rapids: Baker, 1992).

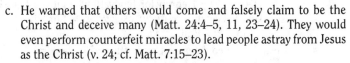

3. Jesus himself claimed to be the Christ.

   a. See Matt. 26:63–65; Mark 14:61–64; 15:2; Luke 4:21; John 4:25–26.

   b. He commended others when they proclaimed him as the Christ (Matt. 16:16–17, 20; John 11:27).

   c. He warned that others would come and falsely claim to be the Christ and deceive many (Matt. 24:4–5, 11, 23–24). They would even perform counterfeit miracles to lead people astray from Jesus as the Christ (v. 24; cf. Matt. 7:15–23).

   d. One must acknowledge Jesus as the Christ in order to be saved (John 11:25–27; Matt. 16:13–20).

4. Many Scriptures show the Christ doing things that a "divine idea" could never do.

   Christ was born (Matt. 1:16; 2:4; Luke 2:11; John 7:42), had human ancestry (Rom. 1:3; 9:5), was from the seed of David (John 7:42), is a Son (Matt. 22:42; Rom. 1:3; Heb. 3:6), has a body (Rom. 7:4; 1 Cor. 10:16; 12:27), had blood (1 Cor. 10:16; Eph. 2:13; Heb. 9:12–14; 1 Peter 1:19; 1 John 1:7), was crucified (1 Cor. 1:23; Gal. 3:13), suffered (Luke 24:26, 46; Acts 3:18; 17:3; 26:23; 1 Peter 1:11; 2:21; 3:18), and was raised from the dead (Acts 26:23; Rom. 6:4; 8:11; 15:12–13; 1 Cor. 15).

5. Jesus claimed to be much more than a Way-shower.

   a. He claimed to be an example (John 13:15), but also much more than that. What gives Eddy the right to selectively use the verses that claim Jesus as an example and ignore the verses in which Jesus claims to be more?

   b. Jesus claimed to be the "way " (John 14:6). There is a big difference between being merely a Way-shower and actually being "the Way." It is analogous to the difference between a road sign that tells of a destination and the road that actually leads to the destination.

D. *Argument Used to Prove the Biblical Doctrine of the Person of Jesus Christ*

1. Jesus claimed to be God himself.

   Jesus used the divine name (Hebrew = *YAHWEH*, Ex. 3:14; Greek = *ego eimi*, "*I AM*") of himself (John 8:24, 28, 58; also John 6:35; 8:12; 9:5; 10:7, 9, 11, 14; 11:25; 14:6; 15:1, 5). In these emphatic self-descriptions Jesus expressed his eternity and oneness of nature with God the Father. (See similar statements in John 13:19; 18:5–6.)

2. Jesus is called fully God in both the Old and New Testaments.

   a. In the New Testament:

      (1) Jesus is called *Theos* (Greek="God") by John (John 1:1, 14), Thomas (John 20:28), the author of Hebrews (Heb. 1:3, 8), Paul (Acts 20:28; Rom. 9:5; Col. 2:9; 1 Tim. 1:16–17), and Peter (Acts 2:34 ff.).

(2) Jesus is called God (*Theos*) and Savior (2 Peter 1:1; Titus 2:13),[101] yet God the Father declares he is the *only* God and Savior (Isa. 45:21–23; also cf. Phil. 2:10–11).

      (3) Jesus was referred to by the Old Testament name for God (*YAHWEH* = Hebrew for Jehovah) when it was translated into Greek (second century) as *Kyrios* = Lord (Rom. 10:9, 13; 1 Cor. 12:3; Phil. 2:11).

   b. Jesus is called *Jehovah God* in the Old Testament:

      (1) God with us (Isa. 7:14 with Matt. 1:23).

      (2) Mighty God and Father (source) of eternity (Isa. 9:6).

      (3) The one to whom every knee will bow as God (Isa. 45:23 cf. Phil. 2:10).

      (4) The eternal one (Mic. 5:2).

      (5) The Creator God (Ps. 102:24–27 with Heb. 1:10–12).

3. Jesus is described as fully man and fully God.

   a. His humanity is seen in his incarnation in the form of a servant (John 14:28; 1 Cor. 3:23; 11:3; 15:24, 28; Phil. 2:6–8; Col. 1:15; 1 Tim. 2:5; Heb. 2:14–18).

   b. He preexisted from all eternity before he became man (Isa. 9:6; Mic. 5:2; John 1:1–2, 15, 30; 3:13; 6:33, 38, 46, 51, 62; 8:23, 42, 58; 16:27–28; 17:5; Col. 1:15; Heb. 1:3; Rev. 1:8).

   c. He uniquely shares the divine nature with the Father; they are one in essence, co-equal, co-eternal, consubstantial (John 1:1; Col. 2:9; Heb. 1:3; Titus 2:13).[102]

   d. Christ was full humanity and full deity in human flesh (John 1:1, 14, 18; 1 John 4:1–3; Phil. 2:5–11; Heb. 2:14–15).

4. Jesus has the attributes and performs the actions of full deity (see Point II.D.2.c–d. above).

5. Jesus proved he is fully God by rising from the dead as he predicted (John 2:19)—(see Point V.C–D below).

6. Jesus is the Christ (see Point III.C.2 above).

IV. The Doctrine of Man

A. The Christian Science Position on Man Briefly Stated

1. Man is God's spiritual idea, individual, yet not material.

2. Man is perfect, without sin, and eternal.

3. Man is a part of God.

---

[101]According to the Granville-Sharp rule of Greek grammar, this construction means that the terms "God" and "Savior" both refer to Jesus.

[102]The term "consubstantial" means "of the same substance." Thus the Father and the Son possess the very same divinity.

B. Arguments Used by Christian Scientists to Support Their Position on Man

1. Man is spiritual, not material.

   a. Because God is All-in-all, man must be a part of Divine Mind.

   b. Man is the compound idea of infinite Spirit and the spiritual image and likeness of God.[103]

   c. Man is God's spiritual idea, or spiritual offspring—individual, yet not material.[104]

   d. The material universe, including mankind, is merely a counterfeit of the true, perfect, spiritual, harmonious, eternal reality, which is God, Mind, Principle.[105]

   e. Man has no separate existence from God, since God is All-in-all. Man is made in the spiritual image and likeness of God and therefore has no brain, blood, bones, or body. Insofar as man is real, he is God, and whatever else is outside this does not exist.[106]

2. Man does not sin, because sin is unreal.

   a. It is wrong to call man a sinner, because he is made in the image and likeness of God, who is perfect. God can be nothing but good and perfect; therefore man cannot sin. Like Divine Mind, man is totally good, perfect, and eternal;[107] he is incapable of sin, sickness, and death.[108]

   b. Sin and evil are unreal, so true spiritual man cannot sin, for it is an error of mortal mind.[109]

   c. Jesus said, "The kingdom of God is within you," showing that all mankind is divine and therefore sinless and eternal.[110]

3. Man is a part of God, because God is All.

   a. Man is a part of God and the full representation of Divine Mind.[111] Eddy wrote, "Love, the divine Principle, is the Father and Mother of the universe, including man."[112]

   b. Man has no existence separate from God, since God is All-in-all. Insofar as man is real, he is God, and whatever else is outside of this does not exist.[113]

---

[103]*S/H*, 591.

[104]*S/H*, 115–116.

[105]*R.D.S.*, 4.

[106]*S/H*, 475.

[107]*S/H*, 302; Mary Baker Eddy, *Unity of Good*, 1908 ed. (Boston: SC Publishing Society), 49 (hereafter cited as *U.O.G.*).

[108]*S/H*, 475.

[109]*U.O.G.*, 52–53.

[110]*S/H*, 475–77.

[111]*S/H*, 591.

[112]*S/H*, 256.

[113]*S/H*, 475.

c. The spiritual man is co-existent and co-eternal with God.[114] As a drop of water becomes one with the ocean, so man is one in nature with Divine Mind.

    d. Jesus said, "The kingdom of God is within you," showing that all mankind is divine and therefore sinless and eternal.[115]

C. *Refutation of Arguments Used By Christian Scientists to Support Their Position on Man*

1. Man is both spiritual and physical.

    a. This is the clear teaching of Scripture (see Point D below).

    b. It is unreasonable and illogical to affirm the biblical passages that teach man's spiritual nature and totally ignore those that teach his physical nature.

    c. Daily experience continually confirms that we are physical as well as spiritual. To deny that we are physical is to deny the obvious.

2. Man is a sinner in action and nature.

    a. God the Father calls us sinners; Jesus called people sinners and stated that he came to save sinners. Paul the Apostle claimed to be the foremost sinner (see Point D below for biblical proof).

    b. The apostle John stated that if we deny our sinfulness, we are self-deceived (1 John 1:8).

    c. Our daily experience and human history continually confirm this plain teaching of the Bible.

    d. Ask Christian Scientists why they carry a set of keys if there is no such thing as sin.

3. Finite man cannot be a part of an infinite God.

    a. The presupposition that all is divine, including man, is a pantheistic teaching found in Hinduism, not in historic Christianity.

    b. The Scriptures throughout affirm a basic distinction, in nature and person, between the Creator and his creation (see biblical proof in Point D below and the earlier discussion in Point II.D.3).

    c. Mankind does not even come close to demonstrating the qualities of a divine nature, in Scripture, history, or everyday life.

D. *Arguments Used to Prove the Biblical Position on Man*

1. Man is a physical and spiritual being.

    a. Man is created in the spiritual image of God (Gen. 1:26–27; 5:1, 3; 9:6; 1 Cor. 11:7), meaning that he is a finite reflection of God's spiritual, moral, and rational nature.[116]

---

[114]*Misc. Writ.*, 79.

[115]*S/H*, 475–77.

[116]R. C. Sproul, *Essential Truths of the Christian Faith* (Wheaton, Ill.: Tyndale, 1992), 131–32.

b. Man was created by God (Ps. 100:3) with a human nature (Acts 14:14–15), made a physical being (Gen. 1:27; 2:7; 2 Cor. 4:16) with finite flesh (Pss. 78:39; 89:48; 1 Cor. 15:47).

c. The only right response to the one true, holy God is humbly to worship him (Ps. 95:6–7), not arrogantly to claim to be part of him.

2. Man is a sinner and, apart from Jesus Christ, is separated from God.

a. Man since the Fall is a sinner by nature (Gen. 3; Jer. 17:9; Mark 7:21–23; Rom. 5:12–21). This means that he has a bias or propensity toward sin.

b. Man is also a sinner by choice (Rom. 7:14–25) and separated from God because of his sinful behavior (Gen. 3:6–7; Rom. 3:9–23; 5:12–14, 18–19; Eph. 2:1).

c. People die because they are sinners (Gen. 2:16–17; Heb. 9:27).

d. Anyone who claims to be without sin is self-deceived (1 John 1:8–10).

e. Jesus acknowledged that people were sinners (Matt. 9:13; Luke 15:7, 10). Indeed, Jesus came into the world to save sinners (Mark 2:17; 1 Tim. 1:15).

3. Man is not divine in nature, nor is he part of God.

a. This is shown in Genesis 1:26–27; 3:5; Numbers 23:19; Isaiah 31:3; Hosea 11:9; Zechariah 12:1; Acts 14:14–15.

b. Satan is the one who tempted mankind with divine qualities (Gen. 3:4–5; Isa. 14:14–15), and God judges all people who claim them (Ezek. 28:9; Acts 12:22–23; Rom. 1:23–25).

V. The Death and Resurrection of Jesus Christ

A. *The Christian Science Position on the Death and Resurrection of Jesus Christ Briefly Stated*

1. Jesus did not die on the cross.
2. There was no bodily resurrection of Jesus.
3. The disciples were mistaken when they thought Jesus had died.

B. *Arguments Used by Christian Scientists to Support Their Position on the Death and Resurrection of Jesus Christ*

1. Jesus did not die on the cross because there is no such thing as death.[117] Death is an unreal illusion of mortal mind.[118]
2. There could be no literal, physical resurrection, because there is no physical death.[119] When the Bible speaks of resurrection, it means

---

[117]*S/H*, 44; 45–46.
[118]*S/H*, 584.
[119]*S/H*, 73; 291.

spiritualization of thought, in which material belief yields to spiritual understanding.[120]

3. The disciples were mistaken when they thought Jesus had died. When Jesus spoke about his resurrection body as "flesh and bone," he was merely accommodating himself to their immature spiritual ideas.[121]

C. Refutation of Arguments Used by Christian Scientists to Support Their Position on the Death and Resurrection of Jesus Christ

1. The Bible teaches that Jesus did actually die physically on the cross.

   a. Many eyewitnesses saw that he was dead.

   b. The death of Jesus upon the cross is thoroughly substantiated from biblical and secular history.[122]

   c. If Eddy's view were true, the Gospel writers had to be lying about Christ's death. To prove this thesis, Christian Scientists must somehow demonstrate that her "revelation" is superior to that of the Bible. This they cannot do.[123]

2. The Bible clearly teaches that Jesus rose physically from the dead.

3. Jesus did not "accommodate" himself to people's immature spiritual ideas.

   a. This would mean that Jesus was deceiving his disciples by making them think he had a body when he really did not.

   b. Jesus (Luke 24:37–39) flatly refuted the idea that he was merely a materialization of a disembodied spirit when he specifically said that spirits do *not* have bodies such as he had.

   c. Eddy's "accommodation" theory assumes that she somehow knew more than the eyewitnesses to the historical event. One must choose between the testimony of many people who were actually in Jerusalem and witnessed these events (Acts 4:14; 26:26) and the claims of one woman who lived eighteen centuries later.

D. Arguments Used to Prove the Biblical Doctrine of the Death and Resurrection of Jesus Christ[124]

1. Jesus did actually die.

   a. Many passages clearly say he died physically (Rom. 5:6, 8; 8:34; 14:9, 15; 1 Cor. 8:11; 15:3; Phil. 2:8).

---

[120]*S/H*, 593.

[121]*S/H*, 44, 313.

[122]For more details read Josh McDowell's *Resurrection Factor* (San Bernardino, Calif.: Here's Life Publishers, 1981), *Evidence That Demands a Verdict* (1972), and *More Evidence That Demands a Verdict* (1975).

[123]See books on biblical reliability and trustworthiness such as Oswald T. Allis, *The Old Testament: Its Claims and Its Critics;* F. F. Bruce, *The New Testament Documents: Are They Reliable?* and *The Books and the Parchments;* Josh McDowell, *Evidence That Demands a Verdict: Historical Evidence for the Christian Faith; More Evidence That Demands a Verdict: Historical Evidences for the Christian Scriptures;* and *More Than a Carpenter.*

[124]For more details read McDowell, *The Resurrection Factor.*

b. Jesus himself prophesied that he would be killed, then raised from the dead on the third day (Matt. 12:38–40; 16:21; Mark 8:31; Luke 9:22; John 2:19–21).

c. The Gospels abound with eyewitness testimonies of the death of Jesus Christ. Both believers and unbelievers alike knew that he was dead (Matt. 27:50–60; Mark 15:37–41; Luke 23:46; John 19:20–34; Acts 2:32; 3:15). Christ's death and resurrection were completely verifiable by anyone in Jerusalem at the time because they were done "in the open" (Acts 26:26; 1 Cor. 15:5–6).

d. There were many proofs and as many as fifteen postresurrection appearances (Matt. 28:9, 16–17; Mark 16:9; Luke 24:13–15, 28–34, 51; John 20:19–27; 21:1–14; Acts 1:3, 9). More than five hundred people saw him at one time (1 Cor. 15:6–8).

e. Eyewitnesses documented their experience in writing (Gal. 1:11–12; 2:2; 2 Peter 1:16; 1 John 1:1; cf. Luke 1:1–4).

2. The historical reality of the death and resurrection of Jesus forms essential twin truths of Christianity.

a. The continuing apostolic testimony and preaching related in Acts always revealed the main message of the death and resurrection of Jesus Christ (Acts 2:23–24, 32; 3:15; 4:2, 10; 5:30–32; 7:52; 13, 17, etc.).

b. The death and bodily resurrection of Jesus Christ are absolutely essential truths for Christianity.

(1) Without these two facts Christianity would be a lie and the greatest hoax of human history (1 Cor. 15:1–4, 14–19; Gal. 2:20–21).

(2) Romans 10:9 states that belief in the bodily resurrection of Jesus is a mandatory condition for salvation.

(3) Paul pointedly states in 1 Corinthians 15 that without the bodily resurrection of Jesus our preaching would be useless (v. 14), our faith is useless (v. 14), the apostles were false witnesses (v. 15), our "faith is futile" (v. 17), we are still in our sins (v. 17), those who have died in Christ are lost (v. 18), and "we are to be pitied more than all men" (v. 19).

VI. The Doctrines of Sin and Salvation

A. The Christian Science Position on Sin and Salvation Briefly Stated

1. Sin, matter, evil, disease, and death are unreal and an illusion.
2. Man already has everlasting salvation; there is no final judgment.
3. We save ourselves; no one else can.
4. Salvation means being saved from the error that sin, sickness, and death exist.

5. Jesus is merely our Way-shower to salvation; he did not pay for sins on the cross.

6. There is no way into the kingdom of heaven except through the practice of CS.

B. *Arguments Used by Christian Scientists to Support Their Position on Sin and Salvation*

1. Sin, matter, evil, disease, and death are unreal and an illusion.

    a. God is good, holy, and perfect, so sin, matter, evil, disease, and death cannot exist, because only Good, God, exists. These "evils" must therefore be unreal and an illusion of mortal mind.[125]

    b. Eddy taught that the way to escape the misery of sin is simply to cease sinning. When we stop believing the lie, error, or belief of sin and begin believing the Truth that sin doesn't exist (because only Divine Mind exists), then we are saved from sin.[126]

2. All will be saved, because nothing exists except God and his ideas.[127]

    a. "Man as God's idea is already saved with an everlasting salvation."[128]

    b. God is perfect love, so there can be no final judgment.[129]

    c. In true reality there is no such thing as separation from God, or hell.[130] Sinners make their own hell by doing or thinking evil, or their own heaven by doing or thinking what is right.[131]

3. Salvation is being saved from the error that sin, sickness, and death exist.

    a. Salvation is being saved from unreal errors of mortal thought.[132]

    b. The source of man's problem is not sin but mortal mind (belief in matter, animal magnetism, or error).[133] To remove the illusion of sin or sickness, one must mentally apply the Spirit of Truth in CS to cast out its error.[134] Then Truth, Spirit, will reign supreme in its absolute perfection, which is salvation.[135]

4. Jesus is merely our Way-shower to salvation; he did not pay for our sins on the cross.

---

[125]*Misc. Writ.*, 27.

[126]*S/H*, 327.

[127]*S/H*, 331; 71.

[128]*Misc. Writ.*, 261.

[129]*S/H*, 291.

[130]*S/H*, 588.

[131]*S/H*, 266.

[132]*S/H*, 593, 468; *Misc. Writ.*, 89.

[133]*S/H*, 591–92.

[134]*S/H*, 130.

[135]*S/H*, 493–95.

a. Jesus is the Way-shower to salvation, meaning that he set an example of how we save ourselves through metaphysics.[136]

b. "Christ came to destroy the belief of sin." Sin, sickness, and death are error.[137]

c. The atonement of Christ reconciles man to God, but not God to man, because the divine Principle of Christ is God. How can God propitiate himself?[138]

d. It is a man-made theory to think that God's wrath could be vented upon his beloved Son.[139]

e. The material blood of Jesus did not and cannot cleanse anyone from sin.[140]

f. It is not the person of Jesus who saves, but the Principle for which he stands.[141]

5. We must save ourselves; no one else can.

a. It is each person's own responsibility, as the Bible says, to "work out your own salvation." Sinners must work out their salvation through sacrifice and right spiritual understanding.[142]

b. Another's vicarious effort, no matter how great, could never pay the debt of sin and do the work we must do for ourselves.[143]

6. There is no way into the kingdom of heaven except through the practice of CS.

a. CS is the "*final* revelation" of God for this age and therefore must be accepted either in this mortal life or after.[144] Christian Science is perfect and divine and completes what Jesus left undone.[145]

b. There is no way into the kingdom of heaven except through the practice of CS.[146] CS has opened the door to human understanding so we may enter the kingdom of God; no one can enter any other way.[147]

c. CS teaches that heaven is the reign of Divine Science.[148]

---

[136]*S/H*, 30, 46, 288, 497.

[137]*S/H*, 473.

[138]*S/H*, 18.

[139]*S/H*, 22–23, 285.

[140]*S/H*, 25.

[141]*S/H*, 146:15ff.

[142]*S/H*, 22, 23.

[143]*S/H*, 18, 22, 23.

[144]*S/H*, 107, emphasis added.

[145]*S/H*, 99, 147.

[146]*CS Journal*, April 1980, 186. CS makes this exclusive claim while at the same time teaching universal salvation. It attempts to resolve this contradiction by stating the belief that all *eventually* (sometime in eternity) will come to accept CS truth.

[147]*S/H*, 99.

[148]*First Church of Christ, Scientist and Miscellany* (Boston: CS Publishing Society, 1913), 267. "Divine Science" means the universal expression of CS; it is the name Eddy gave metaphysical truth before she "discovered" it in 1866.

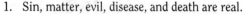

C. Refutation of Arguments Used by Christian Scientists to Support Their Position on Sin and Salvation

1. Sin, matter, evil, disease, and death are real.

   a. The monistic worldview of Eddy gives her a distorted view of sin and salvation. God is good, but it doesn't follow logically that therefore nothing else exists in the universe.

   b. The biblical distinction between a holy Creator God (who is both transcendent and immanent) and his finite creation (Isa. 45:18) solves the problem that sin appears to come from a good God.

      (1) God gave man free moral choice to choose to love his Creator (Gen. 1–3).

      (2) Man has rebelled against God and brought the destruction of his sin upon himself (Rom. 3:23; 5:12; 6:23).

   c. Christ's purpose in coming to earth was to save *real* sinners (1 Tim. 1:15) by *dying* for them on the cross (Matt. 16:21–26; 20:28; John 6:51).

   d. Sin and its destructive effects are very real in history and in everyday experience.

2. The Bible does not teach universal salvation.

   a. It teaches that some will be saved and others will not, by their own choice (Matt. 7:15–23; 24:45–46; John 5:28–29).

   b. Some sin will not be forgiven because of lack of repentance (Matt. 12:30–32).

   c. There will be a final judgment of all people after death by Jesus Christ (Matt. 16:27; Heb. 9:27; Rev. 20:12–13).

   d. There will be eternal punishment for those who reject Jesus Christ and his gospel (2 Thess. 1:8–9; Rev. 19:20; 20:15; 21:8).

3. We cannot save ourselves; only Jesus Christ can save us.

   a. Mankind has a sin problem that he cannot solve himself (Luke 7:37–48).

   b. Throughout Scripture God declares that salvation is a gift that cannot be earned or deserved by any person (Gen. 15:6; Rom. 3:22–24; 9:16; Eph. 2:8–9; Titus 3:5–7).

   c. God's remedy for sin is personally trusting in Jesus Christ alone and his work on the cross (John 3:16; 14:6; Acts 4:12).

   d. The verse that says "work out your own salvation" (Phil. 2:12) interprets itself when it says God makes it possible for one to work (v. 13). The book of Philippians was written to *believers* who already possessed salvation, not unbelievers who needed salvation. Paul is telling these Christians to "work out" their salvation, that is, to show evidence of the salvation they already possess. Good works are not a means to eternal life but an evidence that one pos-

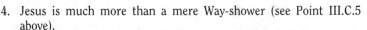

sesses it through faith in Jesus Christ (Rom. 8:3–4; Eph. 2:8–10; James 2:14–26; 1 John 3:9–10).

4. Jesus is much more than a mere Way-shower (see Point III.C.5 above).

D. Arguments Used to Prove the Biblical Doctrine of Sin and Salvation

1. Sin is "missing the mark."

a. The Greek word *harmatia*, translated "sin," means "to miss the mark," as in missing the standard of God's righteousness expressed in his law. Sin is also:

(1) Lawlessness (1 John 3:4)

(2) Transgression of God's law (James 2:11)

(3) Any wrongdoing (1 John 5:17)

b. More technically, sin may be defined as "any want of conformity unto, or transgression of any law of God."[149] Sin is biblically defined as anything that displeases God, in deed (1 John 3:4), omission (James 4:17; Matt. 25:41–46), thought (Prov. 24:9), or word (Matt. 12:37).

2. Sin is universal and very real.

a. All people sin (Rom. 3:23; 1 John 1:8–10; Pss. 130:3; 143:2).

b. All people are sinners by nature.

(1) Through the fall of Adam and Eve (Gen. 3), all people inherit a sinful nature when they are born (called "original sin," seen in Rom. 5:12–21).

(2) We are sinners because we sin; we sin because we are sinners.

c. The natural human heart is deceitful above all things and desperately sick from sin (Jer. 17:9).

d. Unsaved people are slaves of sin (Rom. 7:5, 8, 14–15, 19–24).

e. God tells us to acknowledge and confess sin to him (Pss. 32:5; 38:18; 51:3–4).

3. Sin has destructive results.

a. Sin separates us from God (Rom. 6:23; Eph. 2:1–2; Col. 1:21; 2:13–14; James 2:12–15).

b. Sin causes spiritual bondage and blindness (John 8:34; 9:41).

c. God holds us accountable for our sin, and we suffer the consequences of it (Ex. 32:34).

4. Sin requires payment that we cannot make for ourselves.

a. Human beings can never cancel out their own sin by good works (Rom. 3; James 2:10), nor can they earn or deserve eternal life (Titus 3:5–7; Rom. 9:16). Salvation is a gift (Eph. 2:8–9).

---

[149]*Westminster Larger Catechism,* Question # 24.

    b. Without the shedding of blood there is no forgiveness of sin (Heb. 9:11–22).

5. Jesus Christ paid the penalty for our sins.

    Jesus Christ died for our sins (1 Cor. 15:3), to take their penalty vicariously for us (Isa. 53:5–6, 10; Heb. 9:28; Matt. 26:28) in his body through his blood on the cross (2 Cor. 5:21; Rom. 3:25; 5:9; Eph. 1:7; Col. 1:20–22).

6. Salvation is appropriated by trusting Christ's work of atonement.

    a. There is no other name we can call on to find eternal life, except Jesus Christ (John 10:1–10; 14:6; Acts 4:10–12).

    b. Eternal life is given to those who by grace (Rom. 3:23–24; 11:6) through faith (Rom. 5:1; 10:9–10) trust in Jesus Christ as Savior and Lord (John 3:16).

    c. Those who have personally received him (John 1:12; Rev. 3:20) in this way become adopted children of God (Gal. 4:5; Eph. 1:5).

7. Not all have salvation, and not all will be saved.

    a. God has given eternal life as a gift, and this life is in his Son, Jesus Christ. He who has the Son has this life, but he who does not have the Son of God does not (John 3:36; 1 John 5:10–12).

    b. Some will choose salvation; others will reject it (Dan. 12:2; Matt. 7:13–14, 21–23; 10:15; 25:45–46; Rom. 2:8–9; John 3:16–20, 36; 5:29; Rev. 14:11).

    c. Hell is described as a place of eternal separation from the blessings of God, a place of torment, outer darkness, a lake of fire, as the place of future, conscious punishment for those who reject Jesus Christ and his gospel (Dan. 12:2; Matt. 8:11–12; 10:28; 13:42, 50; 18:8–9; 22:13; 25:41, 46; Mark 9:42–48; Luke 3:17; 16:19–31; Jude 3–13; Rev. 14:9–10; 19:20; 20:10–15; 1 Thess. 4:14; 2 Thess. 2:9).

    d. Heaven is described as a place of eternal fellowship with the triune God; a place with the absence of all that brings pain, sin, sorrow, or death; and a place to enjoy God and his rewards forever (Matt. 25:34, 37; John 3:5, 16, 18, 21; 2 Cor. 5:1–8; Heb. 12:22–24; Rev. 21–22). Not all people will be there (Rev. 14:9–11; 19:20; 22:15).

Section 2: Religious Science

Part I: Introduction

I. Historical Background

A. Ernest S. Holmes, Founder (1887–1960)

1. Holmes was born on January 21, 1887, near Lincoln, Maine.

2. Holmes dropped out of school at age fifteen, describing himself as a nonconformist with an insatiable hunger for truth.

3. He was fascinated with the transcendentalism of Emerson and influenced by friends in Christian Science, Emma Curtis Hopkins (student of Mary Baker Eddy and of Divine Science), and by other metaphysical teachers.

4. Holmes followed his brother Fenwicke to California in 1912 and continued privately to study philosophy, metaphysics, and the power of the mind for health, wealth, and happiness. Ernest began modestly what became a profitable public speaking and writing career.

B. Founding of Religious Science (RS, or Science of Mind)

1. In 1917 the two Holmes brothers founded the Metaphysical Institute in Los Angeles.

2. With no college or theological education Holmes published his first book in 1919, entitled *Creative Mind.*

3. In 1926 he published his best-known volume, the 667-page *Science of Mind,* the standard textbook for all Religious Scientists.

   a. It claims that "Religious Science is a correlation of the laws of science, the opinions of philosophy, and the revelations of religion applied to human needs and the aspirations of man."[150]

   b. It contains many concepts and teachings parallel to other metaphysical teachers that preceded Holmes: P. P. Quimby, Mary Baker Eddy, Emma Curtis Hopkins, Charles and Myrtle Fillmore, and Emanuel Swedenborg.[151]

---

[150]*Religious Science: What it is . . . What it can do for you,* 2.

[151]Emanuel Swedenborg (1688–1772) was a distinguished Swedish scientist turned mystic who claimed to have had a life-changing vision of Christ in 1744. His occultic and metaphysical writings were inspired through dreams, visions, and communication with the spirit world.

41

    c. One friend said, "Dr. Holmes was a natural metaphysician. The writings of Eddy and Judge Troward, he knew backwards and forwards."[152]

4. Holmes incorporated his movement in 1927.

    a. He established headquarters in Los Angeles as "The Institute of Religious Science and School of Philosophy, Inc."

    b. His teaching spread through Sunday morning services and classes.

    c. Holmes sought out university professors as guest speakers for his institute in an effort to legitimize "modern metaphysics."

    d. In 1930 he was promoting RS via a CBS radio program, his first branch church in Hollywood, and his new magazine, *Science of Mind*.

    e. In 1954, the first split in the movement occurred and the International Association of Religious Science Churches broke away from the Institute, still following Holmes's teaching (see Section II.D below under Religious Science International).

    f. The Institute was renamed in 1967 and became known as the United Church of Religious Science.

C. *Characteristics of Religious Science*

1. RS presents itself as a cure-all "philosophy, religion, and science."

2. It claims that by using its way of thinking, understanding, metaphysical principles, and methods one can, as a divine being, become the master of one's own destiny.

3. It promises that by using its teaching and healing techniques, one will experience health, abundance, harmonious relationships, success, creative activity, love, and peace.

4. As a philosophy it asserts a monistic, panentheistic worldview in order to understand the universe and man's relationship to it; therefore it is closer to Hinduism than to Christianity.

5. It uses Christian terminology without biblical content and attempts to merge Christianity with all other religions.

6. To summarize, its approach to reality can be stated as "God, Divine Mind, is the only Power, and Mind expresses itself through our thought."[153]

II. Vital Statistics

A. *Membership Figures*

1. In 1991, the approximate membership for Religious Science was 600,000.[154]

---

[152]Robert H. Bitzer, *A Quick Look at Religious Science International* (Spokane: RSI), 2.

[153]*S/M*, 35, 390–423.

[154]*Orange County Register*, 21 March 1991, E–1.

2. There were 100 chartered churches in the mid-1970s and more than 160 accredited and licensed "practitioners" (those called upon for healing guidance).

3. There were 125 churches by 1988, and in 1993 there were 180 churches and 52 study groups in addition to 47 groups outside the USA.

B. Religious Science Today

1. The movement continues to expand as the fastest-growing mind science group.

   a. It has been popularized by such people as Terry Cole-Whitaker in her Science of Mind Church International.

   b. Whitaker's positive gospel of success has a definite New Age flair and includes "rebirthing,"[155] body massage, nutrition, visualization, channeling, and goddess and Mother Earth energies.[156]

2. It has *not* grown nearly as much as Holmes boasted it would, when he claimed in 1958, "We have launched a Movement which, in the next 100 years, will be the great new religious impulsion of modern times, far exceeding, in its capacity to envelop the world, anything that has happened since Mohammedanism started. It is the only thing that will keep the world from destroying itself."[157]

C. Literature Distribution

1. Main literature includes *The Science of Mind* textbook, *Science of Mind* magazine, and other publications (see Selected Bibliography).

2. Literature is distributed in the USA and at least seventeen other countries.

D. Religious Science International

1. Religious Science International (RSI) has its headquarters in Spokane, Washington, and has fewer members than the original body.

2. RSI was created on May 27, 1949, under the name The International Association of Religious Science Churches.

3. In 1972 it changed its name to Religious Science International.

4. RSI offers its member churches resources for education, training for ministers, and assistance in establishing new churches. It publishes the monthly devotional book *Creative Thought* and *The Reporter* three times each year.

5. Both groups (RS and RSI) promote the teaching of Ernest Holmes and *The Science of Mind.*

---

[155]"Rebirthing" is a healing practice of the New Age movement that involves recalling the moment of birth and releasing its trauma.

[156]William Watson, *A Concise Dictionary of Cults and Religions* (Chicago: Moody Press, 1991), 204.

[157]James Reid, *Ernest Holmes: The First Religious Scientist,* (Los Angeles: Science of the Mind Publications, n.d.), 14.

Part II: Theology

I. The Doctrine of Revelation and Scripture

A. *The Religious Science Position on Revelation and Scripture Briefly Stated*

1. The "Bibles" of every religion are valuable sources of Truth.
2. These sacred writings must be interpreted metaphysically, not literally.
3. Ernest Holmes, above all people, can give the metaphysical understanding to interpret these sacred writings properly.
4. Every person can receive revelations from God for oneself, but not for someone else.
5. Jesus was a master metaphysician who taught these Truths of Divine metaphysics.

B. *Arguments Used by Religious Science to Support Its Position on Revelation and Scripture*[158]

1. The "Bibles" of every religion are valuable sources of Truth.

   a. Religious Science is not a special revelation from God, but a compilation of the best thought of the ages from all religions and philosophies.
   b. RS is based on the Bible and other sacred writings, which virtually teach one and the same Truth. That is, God is the Supreme All and we are one with him.
   c. It is unreasonable to think that any one person or group has a corner on truth for the whole, diverse human race. All religious Truth is one just as God is one.
   d. We believe that the Bible is important, but equally valuable are all the other revelations God has given to mankind, such as the *Text of Taoism*, the *Sacred Books of the East*, the *Zend-Avesta*, the *Koran*, the teachings of Buddha, the *Apocrypha*, the *Talmud*, *The Awakening of Faith*, the *Echoes From Gnosis*, *Fragments of a Forgotten Faith*, *Ramacharaka*, the *Bhagavad-Gita*, the *Vedas*, including the *Upanishads*, the *Pistis Sophia*, *The Book of the Dead*, the *Qabbalah*, the *Hermetic Philosophy*, and, of course, *The Science of Mind* by Ernest Holmes, who helps us to synthesize and interpret all these other revelations correctly.
   e. "It borrows much of its light from others but, in so doing, robs no one, for Truth is universal. The Christian Bible, perhaps the greatest book ever written, truly points a way to eternal values. But

---

[158]Note that some of the arguments used by Religious Science are virtually the same as those used in Christian Science. See Part II, Point I.B. under Christian Science. RS does differ in that it recognizes all religious writings as equal.

there are many other bibles, all of which, taken together, weave the story of spiritual Truth into a unified pattern. It is unreasonable to suppose that any one person, or race, encompasses all truth, and alone can reveal the way of life to others. Taking the best from all sources, Religious Science has access to the highest enlightenment of the ages. **Religious Science reads everyman's Bible and gleans the truths therein contained.** It studies all peoples' thought and draws from each that which is true."[159]

f. "God has been called by a thousand different names throughout the ages. The time has now come to cast aside any points of disagreement and to realize that we are all worshiping one and the same God."[160]

2. These sacred writings must be interpreted metaphysically, not literally.

   a. To understand the true, spiritual interpretation of all these writings properly, one needs Religious Science's understanding of Truth.

   b. "BIBLE: Do we use it? Of course. Do we take it literally? No. Truth is Truth and the Bible must be read with an open mind, looking for the higher meaning in the stories, metaphors, and parables."[161]

3. Ernest Holmes, above all people, can give the metaphysical understanding to interpret these sacred writings properly.

   a. "The Science of Mind is not a special revelation of any individual; it is, rather, the culmination of all revelations."[162]

   b. Ernest Holmes has done the best job of synthesizing the Truth found in all religions. As the first Religious Scientist, he best explained the infallibility of the laws of the universe.

   "He sought only to explain the infallibility of the laws and express the essence of the ever-existent way. *No one* before him had done that. His work was to make this modest man 'a man for the ages'— a *pioneering guide to all mankind*. His name was Ernest Holmes."[163]

   c. Holmes became an authority on the universal truths of the ages expressed in literature, art, science, philosophy, and religion.[164]

4. Every person can receive revelations from God for oneself, but not for someone else.

   a. Any person can do what Jesus did and receive revelation from God and then choose to live up to it. God is no respecter of persons.

[159]Ernest Holmes, *What Religion Science Teaches* (Los Angeles: Science of the Mind Publications), 9, their emphasis.

[160]*What RS Teaches*, 28.

[161]Dennis M. Jones, *How to Speak Religious Science* (Spokane: RSI), 2.

[162]Ernest Holmes, *The Science of Mind* (New York: Dodd, Mead, 1965), 35 (hereafter cited as *S/M*).

[163]Reid, *Ernest Holmes: The First Religious Scientist*, 1–2; italics added.

[164]Reid, *Ernest Holmes: The First Religious Scientist*, 2.

b. Each person must receive revelation for oneself. Jesus taught that the human mind and God's Mind are one and the same. Therefore, we can be in direct contact with God as Jesus was.

c. "REVELATION—becoming consciously aware of hidden things. Since the mind that man uses is the same Mind that God uses, the One and Only Mind, the avenues of Revelation can never be closed. But no man can receive the Revelation for another."[165]

d. "While I believe in other men's revelations, I am sure only of my own."[166]

5. Jesus was a master metaphysician who taught these Truths of Divine metaphysics.

a. Jesus understood and taught the eternal truths of spiritual mind healing; he taught that whatever he did, we could do.

b. His parables and healing miracles are proof of this.

c. "Jesus, the last of his particular line of prophets, was the first to introduce spiritual mind healing, and definitely to instruct his followers to practice it."[167]

C. *Refutation of Arguments Used by Religious Science to Support Its Position on Revelation and Scripture*[168]

1. The Bible is complete and final; therefore another "revelation" is not needed.

2. The metaphysical interpretation of the Bible is totally subjective, unverifiable, and therefore useless.

3. A metaphysical interpretation of the Bible is not needed.

a. The writers of the Bible did not interpret other passages of the Scripture metaphysically, but rather literally, historically, normally, in their ordinary, plain sense, *as written.*

b. Jesus did not interpret the Old Testament metaphysically, but rather literally, historically, normally, in its ordinary, plain sense, *as it was written.*

c. The Bible is a self-interpreting book, not needing another, external, authoritative worldview to explain it properly.

4. Ernest Holmes's position on "other sacred writings" is untenable and misleading.

a. The many so-called sacred revelations that claim to be from God do not all agree with Religious Science. Holmes makes them appear to agree by taking them out of context.

---

[165]*S/M*, 630.

[166]*S/M*, 386.

[167]*What RS Teaches*, 75.

[168]Note that since some of the arguments used by Religious Science are virtually the same as those used in Christian Science, some of the refutations remain the same. See Part II, Point I.C under CS. Differences for RS, which uses other sacred writings, are refuted here.

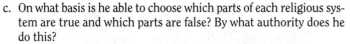

    b. If Holmes claims he did not receive a revelation from God himself, but has compiled all the best truth from all religions, how do we know *objectively* that he has put them together in a way that represents final truth?

    c. On what basis is he able to choose which parts of each religious system are true and which parts are false? By what authority does he do this?

    d. The only religions that can possibly agree with his system are those having the same monistic worldview. This excludes from the outset Christianity, Judaism, Islam, and a host of other religions.

    e. In reality, Holmes's system is merely mind science metaphysics. He finds quotes in other religious works that seem to agree on the surface with his own mind science theology, but which in fact disagree fundamentally with his system.

5. The God of the Bible does not accept all religions and therefore does not accept their so-called written revelations.

    a. Religions do not all agree on the nature of God, the person of Jesus Christ, and the way of salvation; many views are contradictory and therefore cannot all be correct.

       (1) All other religions apart from Christianity deny the Trinity, the deity of Christ, his bodily resurrection, and salvation by grace through faith in the work of Jesus Christ on the cross.

       (2) The pantheism of Eastern religions and the mind sciences contradicts the transcendent and immanent nature of the God of Christianity.

       (3) Non-Christian religions, which reject the adequate revelation God has given of himself, end up rejecting God himself. Therefore it is impossible to harmonize all religions and their contradictory sacred writings.

    b. The exclusive claims of Jesus Christ and his apostles set Christianity apart from all other religions (John 14:6; Acts 4:12; 1 Tim. 2:5); Christianity claims to be the *only* way that God has chosen for people to be reconciled to him.

D. Arguments Used to Prove the Biblical Doctrine of Revelation and Scripture[169]

1. The Bible claims to be reliable and authoritative.

2. The Bible is complete and final.

3. Jesus and the New Testament writers consistently interpreted the Old Testament literally.

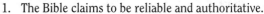

[169]Note that the biblical arguments used to answer the RS teaching on Revelation and Scripture have been included in the CS section. See Part II, Point I.D in CS.

47

II. The Doctrine of God and the Trinity

A. *The Religious Science Position on God and the Trinity Briefly Stated*

1. God is an Impersonal and Universal Principle, Mind, or Idea.

2. God is an Infinite Presence that becomes personalized in, to, and through each human being.

3. God is All, and All is God (All is One).

4. The universe is the Body of God. He is in everything and greater than everything.

5. The Trinity is Spirit, Soul, and Body—a Trinity of Being that includes Man.

6. The Holy Spirit is an impersonal force within mankind that assists us to comprehend metaphysical truth and our oneness with the Divine.

B. *Arguments Used by Religious Science to Support Its Position on God and the Trinity*[170]

1. God is an Impersonal and Universal Principle, Mind, or Idea.

   a. "God is not a person but a Principle personified in each of us."[171]

   b. "The Bible says: 'In Him we live and move and have our being.' . . . 'Him' . . . 'It' . . . 'God.' Jesus said Reality is not in the mountain, nor afar off, but within us. So . . . we make a simple statement: 'Mind is.' Mind is, and Mind is both Universal and individual, i.e., it is not only Universal and abstract, it is also individual and concrete. The Mind which is personified is the same Mind which is Universal."[172]

2. God is an Infinite Presence that becomes personalized in, to, and through each human being.

   a. "God is not a person; God is a Presence personified in us."[173]

   b. "We begin to see that there is an Infinite Personalness . . . where our life is personified, God is personified. If man did not exist, God would be impersonal!"[174]

   c. "In each one of us, to each one of us, through each one of us, something is personalized, and *that which is personalized is personal to its own personification!* "[175]

3. God is All, and All is God (All is One).

   a. "ALL THERE REALLY IS, IS GOD!"[176]

---

[170]Note that some of the arguments used by Religious Science are virtually the same as those used in Christian Science. See Part II, Point II.B under CS.

[171]*S/M*, 621.

[172]*S/M*, 76.

[173]*S/M*, 308.

[174]*Words That Heal Today*, 6.

[175]*S/M*, 89.

[176]*S/M*, 188.

b. "God is 'All in all.' That is, God IS, and is *in* everything."[177]

c. "The Mind which is personified is the same Mind which is Universal. This is the perception that Buddha, Jesus and other great spiritual leaders had. They understood that the Universe *has* to be *One* in order to be at all."[178]

4. The universe is the Body of God. He is in everything and greater than everything.

a. "THE ENTIRE MANIFESTATION OF SPIRIT, BOTH VISIBLE AND INVISIBLE, IS THE BODY OF GOD. . . . The word 'body' as used in the Science of Mind means all objective manifestations of the invisible Principle of Life. The physical universe is the Body of God—the invisible Principle of all life."[179]

b. "God not only is *in everything, but He is more than everything He is in*! 'Ye are the light of the world.' All that we are is God, yet God is more than all we are."[180]

5. The Trinity is Spirit, Soul, and Body—a Trinity of Being that includes Man.

"Turn it as we may, we are confronted with the necessity of a Trinity of Being. Throughout the ages, this Trinity has been taught. Every great religion and every great spiritual philosophy has taught this Trinity. Father, Son, and Holy Ghost is the Christian Trinity. It is the Thing, the Way it Works, and What it Does. The Thing is Absolute Intelligence; the *way* It works, is Absolute Law; and What It does, is the result—manifestation. The action of the Thing Itself is what the Bible calls 'The Word.' . . . Absolute Intelligence."[181]

6. The Holy Spirit is an impersonal force within all mankind that assists us to comprehend metaphysical truth and our oneness with the Divine.

a. "We are using the word 'Soul' in the sense of a Universal Soul, or Medium, through which Spirit operates. It is the Holy Ghost, or Third Person of the Christian Trinity."[182]

b. "Let us bear in mind that neither Spirit nor the Soul of the Universe were ever created. Each is eternal. Because this impartial, impersonal Soul is the medium through which Spirit works, and because It is a 'blind force not knowing, only doing,' It was called by the ancients 'Maya,' from which arose the teachings of illusions of the mind—the mirror of the mind."[183]

---

177 *S/M*, 103.
178 *S/M*, 76.
179 *S/M*, 98.
180 *S/M*, 362.
181 *S/M*, 80.
182 *S/M*, 90.
183 *S/M*, 93.

   c. "The Holy Comforter, The Spirit of Truth . . . is in all people—not unto Jesus alone—but unto all alike."[184]

C. *Refutation of Arguments Used by Religious Science to Support Its Position on God and the Trinity*[185]

  1. The God of the Bible is a personal being, not an impersonal Principle or "It."

  2. The God of the Bible is a Triune Being: Father, Son, and Holy Spirit.

  3. The God of the Bible is not panentheistic, but is both transcendent and immanent.

   Panentheism (Greek: *pan*, "everything"; *en*, "in"; *theos*, "god") is the belief that God includes and permeates the material world, sometimes expressed as "the universe is God's body." This view is clearly contrary to the biblical teaching about God.

  4. The Bible does not teach monism (all is one).

  5. The Bible teaches that the Holy Spirit is the eternal third person of the Holy Trinity.

D. *Arguments Used to Prove the Biblical Doctrine of God and the Trinity*[186]

  1. The God of the Bible is personal.

  2. The God of the Bible is triune.

  3. God is above and separate from his creation, yet active in it.

  4. The Holy Spirit is the eternal third person of the triune God.

III. The Person of Jesus Christ

A. *The Religious Science Position on Jesus Christ Briefly Stated*

  1. Jesus was a man who had a divinity that all men have.

  2. Jesus was not the Christ, but became the Christ, as we all can become.

  3. The Christ is the eternal Higher Self of every individual.

B. *Arguments Used by Religious Science to Support Its Position on Jesus Christ*[187]

  1. Jesus was a man who had a divinity that all men have.

   a. "Mental Science does not deny the divinity of Jesus, but it does affirm the divinity of all people. It does not deny that Jesus was the Son of God; but it affirms that all men are sons of God."[188]

---

[184]*S/M*, 480.

[185]Note that since the arguments used by Religious Science are virtually the same as those used in Christian Science, the refutations remain the same. See Part II, Point II.C under CS.

[186]Note that since the arguments used by Religious Science are virtually the same as those used in Christian Science, the biblical arguments against the view are the same. Please refer to Part II, Point II.D under CS.

[187]Note that many of the arguments used by Religious Science are virtually the same as those used in Christian Science. See Part II, Point III.B under CS.

[188]*S/M*, 161–62.

b. "To think of Jesus as being different from other men is to misunderstand His mission and purpose in life. *He was a Way-shower and proved His way to be a correct one!*"[189]

2. Jesus was not the Christ, but became the Christ, as we all can become.

   a. "JESUS—the name of a man. Distinguished from the Christ. The man Jesus became the embodiment of the Christ, as the human gave way to the Divine Idea of Sonship."[190]

   b. "In studying the life and teachings of Jesus, the most unique character of history, we discover a few simple ideas underlying his philosophy, the embodiment of which enabled him to become the Christ."[191]

   c. "Jesus never thought of Himself as different from others. His whole teaching was that what He did, others could do."[192]

   d. "Who is Christ? . . . The mystical conception of Christ means the Universality of Sonship, *embodied in any individual who recognizes this Sonship.*"[193]

   e. "Every man is a potential Christ."[194]

3. The Christ is the eternal Higher Self of every individual.

   a. "Christ is the unseen principle in Man. . . . Christ is the reality of every man, his true inner self."[195]

   b. "Christ is Universal Idea . . . the Higher Self."[196]

C. *Refutation of Arguments Used by Religious Science to Support Its Position on Jesus Christ*[197]

1. Jesus is fully human, but he is also fully God (see Point D below).

2. Jesus is explicitly called "the Christ" many times.

3. Jesus himself claimed to be the Christ.

4. Many passages of Scripture show the Christ doing things that a "divine idea" could never do.

5. Jesus claimed to be much more than a Way-shower.

D. *Arguments Used to Prove the Biblical Doctrine of Jesus Christ*[198]

1. Jesus claimed to be God himself.

---

[189]*S/M*, 367.

[190]*S/M*, 603.

[191]*S/M*, 363.

[192]*S/M*, 361–62.

[193]*S/M*, 357.

[194]*What RS Teaches*, 20.

[195]*What RS Teaches*, 12.

[196]*What RS Teaches*, 55.

[197]Note that since the arguments used by Religious Science are virtually the same as those used in Christian Science, the refutations remain the same. See Part II, Point III.C under CS.

[198]Note that since the arguments used by Religious Science are virtually the same as those used in Christian Science, the biblical arguments against them remain the same. See Part II, Point III.D under CS.

2. Jesus is called fully God by others in both the Old and New Testaments.

3. Jesus is described as fully man and fully God.

4. Jesus has the attributes and performs the actions of full deity.

5. Jesus proved he is fully God by rising from the dead as he predicted (John 2:19).

6. Jesus is the Christ.

IV. The Doctrine of Man

A. The Religious Science Position on Man Briefly Stated

1. Man is basically good and does not sin, because sin is unreal; however, he sometimes makes mistakes.

2. Man is a part of God, because God is All. Man is Divine and One with God in true reality; he is a microcosm or miniature of God.

3. Man must overcome his ignorance of his oneness with Divine Mind and become Christ.

B. Arguments Used by Religious Science to Support Its Position on Man[199]

1. Man is basically good and does not sin, because sin is unreal; however, he sometimes makes mistakes.

   "SIN—We have tried to show that there is no sin but a mistake, and no punishment but a consequence. The Law of cause and effect. Sin is merely missing the mark. God does not punish sin. As we correct our mistakes, we forgive our own sins."[200]

2. Man is a part of God, because God is All. Man is Divine and One with God in true reality; he is a microcosm or miniature of God.

   a. "We shall see in everyone a budding genius, a becoming God, an unfolding soul, an eternal destiny."[201]

   b. "This makes of the human being a Divine being, a personification of the Infinite."[202]

   c. "There is that within us which partakes of the nature of the Divine Being, and since it partakes of the nature of the Divine Being, we are divine."[203]

   d. "The Divine Incarnation is inherent in our nature."[204]

---

[199]Note that arguments used by Religious Science are virtually the same as those used in Christian Science. See Part II, Point IV.B under CS.

[200]*S/M*, 633.

[201]*S/M*, 387.

[202]*What I Believe*, 3.

[203]*S/M*, 33–34.

[204]*S/M*, 42.

3. Man must overcome his ignorance of his oneness with Divine Mind and become Christ.

a. "Not some men, but all men, are divine. But all men have not yet recognized their divinity."[205]

b. "There is something Divine about us which we have overlooked. There is more to us than we realize. Man is an eternal destiny, a forever-expanding principle of conscious intelligence . . . the ocean in the drop of water, the sun in its rays. Man, the real man, is birthless, deathless, changeless; and God, as man, in man, IS man!"[206]

c. "When any individual recognizes his true union with the Infinite, he automatically becomes the Christ."[207]

C. *Refutation of Arguments Used by Religious Science to Support Its Position on Man*[208]

1. Man is both spiritual and physical.

2. Man is a sinner in nature and in deed.

3. Finite man cannot be a part of an infinite God.

D. *Arguments Used to Prove the Biblical Doctrine of Man*[209]

1. Man is a physical and spiritual being.

2. Man is a sinner and, apart from Jesus Christ, is separated from God.

3. Man is not divine in nature, nor is he part of God.

V. The Death and Resurrection of Jesus Christ

A. *The Religious Science Position on the Death and Resurrection of Jesus Christ Briefly Stated*

1. Jesus did not die on the cross, because there is no death.

2. There was no bodily resurrection of Jesus.

B. *Arguments Used by Religious Science to Support Its Position on the Death and Resurrection of Jesus Christ*[210]

1. Jesus could not have died, because there is no death.

a. "The resurrection is the death of the belief that we are separated from God. For death is to the illusion alone and not to Reality. God

[205]*What RS Teaches,* 57.

[206]*S/M,* 388.

[207]*What RS Teaches,* 65.

[208]Note that since the arguments used by Religious Science are virtually the same as those used in Christian Science, the refutations remain the same. See Part II, Point IV.C under CS.

[209]Note that since the arguments used by Religious Science are virtually the same as those used in Christian Science, the biblical arguments remain the same. See Part II, Point IV.D under CS.

[210]Note that arguments used by Religious Science are virtually the same as those used in Christian Science. See Part II, Point V.B under CS.

did not die. What happened was that man awoke to Life. The awakening must be on the part of man since God already is Life."[211]

    b. "There is every reason to suppose that we have a body within a body to infinity, and it is our belief that we do have. The 'resurrection body,' then, will not be snatched from some Cosmic Shelf, as the soul soars aloft. It is already *within* and we may be certain that it will be a fit instrument for the future unfoldment of the soul. It would seem, then, that we have a spiritual body now, and need not die to receive one. If there are many planes of Life and consciousness as we firmly believe, perhaps we only die from one plane to another."[212]

2. There was no bodily resurrection of Jesus.

    a. There could be no literal physical resurrection, because there is no physical death. Resurrection means a spiritualization of thought by our overcoming false beliefs about death and realizing our perfection. "Resurrection—Rising from a belief in death."[213]

    b. "The physical disappearance of Jesus after His resurrection was the result of the spiritualization of His consciousness. This so quickened His mentality that His body disintegrated and His followers could not see Him because He was on another plane. Planes are not places; they are states of consciousness."[214]

    c. "Jesus revealed himself to his followers after his resurrection, *to show them that death is but a passing to a higher sphere of life and action*."[215]

C. *Refutation of Arguments Used by Religious Science to Support Its Position on the Death and Resurrection of Jesus Christ*[216]

1. The Bible teaches that Jesus actually died physically on the cross (see the biblical proof in Section D below).

2. The Bible teaches that Jesus rose physically from the dead.

D. *Arguments Used to Prove the Biblical Doctrine of the Death and Resurrection of Jesus Christ*[217]

1. Jesus actually died.

2. The historical reality of the death and resurrection of Jesus forms essential twin truths of Christianity.

---

[211]*S/M*, 413.

[212]*S/M*, 376.

[213]*S/M*, 630.

[214]*S/M*, 104.

[215]*S/M*, 377.

[216]Note that since the arguments used by Religious Science are virtually the same as those used in Christian Science, the refutations remain the same. See Part II, Point V.C under CS.

[217]Note that since the arguments used by Religious Science are virtually the same as those used in Christian Science, the biblical arguments remain the same. See Part II, Point V.D under CS.

VI. The Doctrines of Sin and Salvation

A. *The Religious Science Position on Sin and Salvation Briefly Stated*

1. Sin, evil, disease, and death are unreal and an illusion.
2. Man already has everlasting salvation; there is no final judgment.
3. We save ourselves; no one else can.
4. Salvation is being saved from the error that sin, sickness, and death exist.
5. Jesus is merely our Way-shower to salvation, not our Redeemer.

B. *Arguments Used by Religious Science to Support Its Position on Sin and Salvation*[218]

1. Sin, evil, disease, and death are unreal and an illusion.

   a. Sin, matter, evil, disease, and death are unreal and an illusion because All is God.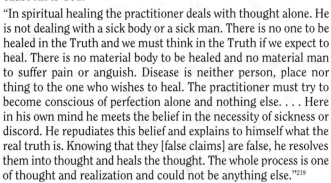

   "In spiritual healing the practitioner deals with thought alone. He is not dealing with a sick body or a sick man. There is no one to be healed in the Truth and we must think in the Truth if we expect to heal. There is no material body to be healed and no material man to suffer pain or anguish. Disease is neither person, place nor thing to the one who wishes to heal. The practitioner must try to become conscious of perfection alone and nothing else. . . . Here in his own mind he meets the belief in the necessity of sickness or discord. He repudiates this belief and explains to himself what the real truth is. Knowing that they [false claims] are false, he resolves them into thought and heals the thought. The whole process is one of thought and realization and could not be anything else."[219]

   b. "All apparent evil is the result of ignorance, and will disappear to the degree that it is no longer thought about, believed in, or indulged in. Evil is not a thing in itself. It has no entity and no real law to support it."[220]

   c. "The conviction that heals is that God is all in all and that there is no material cause or effect. The practitioner treats, not a patient nor a disease; he seeks to heal the thought of its mistaken idea that causation is independent of good. To do this he must contradict what appears to be so."[221]

2. Man already has everlasting salvation; there is no final judgment.

   a. All will be saved because nothing exists except God and his ideas.

---

[218]Note that arguments used by Religious Science are virtually the same as those used in Christian Science. See Part II, Point VI.B under CS.

[219]*S/M*, 408–9.

[220]*What RS Teaches*, 13.

[221]*S/M*, 413.

"We need fear nothing in the Universe. We need not be afraid of God. We may be certain that all will arrive at the final goal, that not one will be missing. Every man is an incarnation of God. The soul can no more be lost than God could be lost. We should neither be disturbed by the wailing of prophets, nor the anathemas of theology. What more can life demand of us than that we do the best that we can and try to improve? If we have done this, we have done well and all will be right with our souls both here and hereafter. This leaves us free to work out our own salvation."[222]

b. "No man need prepare to meet his God, he is meeting Him every day and each hour in the day."[223]

c. "Sin is merely missing the mark. God does not punish sin. As we correct our mistakes, we forgive our own sins."[224]

d. "In the long run each will fully express his divinity, for '*good will come at last alike to all.*' We stand in the shadow of a mighty Presence while love forever points the way to heaven."[225]

e. "To believe in eternal damnation for any soul is to believe in an infinite monstrosity, contradicting the integrity of the universe, and repudiating any eternal loving-kindness inherent in God."[226]

f. "Did Jesus die to save us? . . . [Science of Mind] does not teach that Jesus died to assure us of what is already ours. It is not necessary to save something that is not lost."[227]

3. Salvation is achieved by recognizing our unity with the Divine.

a. "Heaven and hell are states of consciousness in which we now live according to our own state of understanding. In the long run, all will be saved from themselves through their own discovery of their Divine nature, and this is the only salvation necessary and the only one that could really be."[228]

b. "The problem of good and evil will never enter the mind which is at peace with itself. When we make mistakes, we suffer the consequences. When, by reason of enlightenment and understanding, we correct such mistakes, we no longer suffer from them. Understanding alone constitutes true salvation, either here or hereafter."[229]

---

[222]*S/M*, 383–84.

[223]*S/M*, 388.

[224]*S/M*, 633.

[225]*What RS Teaches*, 21, italics added.

[226]Holmes, *The Essence of Science of Mind*, 14.

[227]Margaret R. Stortz, *What Science of Mind Is All About* (Los Angeles: Science of Mind Publ., n.d.),6.

[228]Ernest Holmes, *What I Believe*, 6.

[229]*S/M*, 383.

   c. "Salvation is not a thing, not an end, but a Way. The way of salvation is through man's unity with the Whole."[230]

4. We save ourselves; no one else can.

   "If you can accept the idea that God is within you, you have made a great start toward feeling and realizing the Presence of God. It is strictly a do-it-yourself operation. It takes thought and reflection . . . asking questions . . . reading . . . meditation and the use of scientific prayer called spiritual mind treatment."[231]

5. Jesus is merely our Way-shower to salvation, not our Redeemer.

   a. "SAVIOR: Is Jesus our saviour? No. Jesus was a wayshower and master teacher who knew the Divine Truth about himself and all others. We do not believe he died on a cross to save us from sin."[232]

   b. "Science of Mind indicates that through his teachings Jesus showed that we are eternal beings, able to live happier, more creative lives. In using these teachings we can be saved from suffering many of life's miseries."[233]

C. Refutation of Arguments Used by Religious Science to Support Its Position on Sin and Salvation[234]

1. Sin, matter, evil, disease, and death are real.

2. The Bible does not teach universal salvation.

3. We cannot save ourselves; only Jesus Christ can.

4. Jesus is much more than a mere Way-shower.

D. Arguments Used to Prove the Biblical Doctrines of Sin and Salvation[235]

1. Sin is "missing the mark." It is anything that displeases God in thought, word, and deed.

2. Sin is universal and very real.

3. Sin has destructive results.

4. Sin requires payment that we cannot make for ourselves.

5. Jesus Christ paid the penalty for our sins.

6. Salvation is appropriated by trusting Christ's work of atonement.

7. Not all have salvation, and not all will be saved.

---

[230]*S/M*, 631.

[231]Margaret R. Stortz, *Science of Mind and God* (Los Angeles: Science of Mind Publ., n.d.), 6.

[232]Jones, *How To Speak Religious Science*, 5.

[233]Stortz, *What Science of Mind Is All About*, 6.

[234]Note that since the arguments used by Religious Science are virtually the same as those used in Christian Science, the refutations remain the same. See Part II, Point VI.C under CS.

[235]Note that since the arguments used by Religious Science are virtually the same as those used in Christian Science, the biblical arguments remain the same. See Part II, Point VI.D under CS.

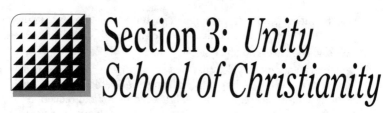

Section 3: *Unity School of Christianity*

Part I: Introduction

I. History

A. *Charles Sherlock Fillmore (1854–1948) and His Wife Myrtle (1845–1931), Founders of Unity School of Christianity (USC)*

   1. Charles and Myrtle both claimed to have experienced ill health as children.

      a. Myrtle Page was reared by Methodist parents and "had been brought up in the belief that she was an invalid and had inherited a tendency to tuberculosis."[236] She also suffered from malaria.[237]

      b. At the age of ten, Charles was in a skating accident that dislocated and diseased his hip, resulting in a withered leg.

   2. Myrtle began a teaching career while Charles eventually went into the real estate business.

   3. They met in 1876 and were married in a Methodist church in Clinton, Missouri, in 1881.

   4. They had three children: Lowell, Waldo, and Royal.

B. *Myrtle's Desperate Search and Her "Discovery"*

   1. Her encounter with Dr. Weeks

      a. When Myrtle's tuberculosis grew worse in 1886, she attended a lecture in Kansas City given by Dr. Eugene B. Weeks of the Illinois Metaphysical College, founded by Emma Curtis Hopkins.[238]

      b. Dr. Weeks's series of talks on metaphysics was variously called "New Thought," "Christian Science," and "Divine Science."

      c. Myrtle was so desperate for healing that "they had reached the place where they were willing to try anything."[239]

---

[236]James D. Freeman, *The Story of Unity* (Lee's Summit, Mo.: Unity School of Christianity, 1954), 29–30.

[237]Freeman, *The Story of Unity*, 39.

[238]Emma Curtis Hopkins was the former editor of Eddy's *Christian Science Journal*. After breaking with Eddy over irreconcilable differences, she founded her own metaphysical school and influenced many of the future founders of metaphysical movements. See Mrs. Hopkins under Religious Science, Part I, Point I.A –B.

[239]Freeman, *The Story of Unity*, 42–44

     d. Myrtle claimed she heard the following statement in Dr. Weeks's lecture that would change her life and become the "seed" from which the Unity movement would grow: "I am a child of God and therefore I do not inherit sickness."

     e. Myrtle began repeating this statement for a period of two years and thereby claimed to be completely healed of all disease.

  2. Her amazing "discovery"

     a. Just like Mrs. Eddy, Myrtle claimed to have made a wonderful metaphysical "discovery," which led to her healing and which she now wanted to share with the world.[240]

     b. Her "discovery" was her method of metaphysical healing that enabled her to "talk to the life in every part of my body and have it do just what I wanted."

     c. After her healing, Myrtle immersed herself in the metaphysical literature of her day, including New Thought, Christian Science, and Divine Science. She also became a good friend and student of Mrs. Hopkins.

     d. Following after Mary Baker Eddy and others, Myrtle claimed the ability to heal through the power of the mind and the "truth" that God is Impersonal Mind.

C. *Charles's Search*

  1. Charles was a confirmed agnostic who, though skeptical at first about his wife's claims and teaching, began to study metaphysics, religions, philosophies, and Eastern and occultic thought. He and his wife to took more than forty courses in metaphysics.[241]

  2. In his search Charles was influenced by Ralph Waldo Emerson (1803–1882) and the Transcendentalists of that day, Emma Curtis Hopkins, Hinduism, Theosophy, Rosicrucianism, Spiritualism, Christian Science, and New Thought.

  3. The Fillmores began to hold twice-weekly meetings to share their eclectic philosophy with others.

  4. Together they developed a "practical and positive" metaphysical teaching that promised unlimited health, happiness, and prosperity.

D. *The Expansion of Unity*

  1. Its eclectic formation

     a. Between 1887 and 1890, the Fillmores were directly associated with the New Thought groups.

     b. In April 1889 Charles began to publish his views in a monthly magazine entitled *Modern Thought.*

---

[240]See the Christian Science Section, Part I, Point I.C.
[241]Freeman, *The Story of Unity*, 41.

(1) In 1891 he changed the name of the journal to *Christian Science Thought*. The name was changed to *Thought* owing to the objections of Mary Baker Eddy.

(2) Early issues had contributions by Christian Scientists, Spiritualists, and Theosophists and articles from occult magazines.

c. The movement was named in 1891 when Charles claimed to have a mystical revelation where he heard the name "UNITY" that "came right out of the ether, just as the voice of Jesus was heard by Paul."

d. He described its eclectic nature and exclusive claims when he wrote, "We have studied many isms, many cults. People of every religion under the sun claim that we either belong to them or have borrowed the best part of our teaching from them. We have borrowed the best from all religions, *that is the reason we are called Unity*. . . . Unity is the Truth that is taught in all religions. . . . The church needs the vitalization that this *renaissance of primitive Christianity* gives it."[242]

2. Outreach and growth of Unity

a. In 1890 The Society of Silent Help was formed, which became the profitable prayer ministry called Silent Unity. In 1910 Silent-70 was created as an outreach to distribute free Unity literature.[243]

b. In 1891 Charles encouraged small "societies" of Unity followers to meet across the nation, and in five years more than 6,000 memberships were issued, 10,000 by 1903, and 15,000 by 1906.

c. Magazines were created as "literature missionaries": *Wee Wisdom* for children (1893), *Unity Daily Word* (1924; now *Daily Word*), *Weekly Unity* (1909), *The Christian Business Man* (1922; incorporated later into *Unity*), and *Youth* (1927; later *Progress*, now *You*).

d. In 1893, at the Columbian exposition in Chicago, the Fillmores met and became admirers of Swami Vivekananda of India, a pioneer of Yogaism in the U.S. As a result, Charles soon incorporated many Hindu and Yoga ideas into Unity, such as reincarnation, vegetarianism, and Eastern philosophy.[244]

e. By 1910, when Unity needed finances to expand its facilities, the Fillmores began to emphasize prayers for prosperity, claiming that God wanted his children to be wealthy. Charles wrote articles such as "Overcoming the Poverty Idea," and Unity's income did grow.

f. In 1914, USC was incorporated and finally in 1922 it dropped its membership in the International New Thought Alliance.[245]

---

[242]Freeman, *The Story of Unity*, 61, italics added.

[243]The name "Silent–70" comes from the seventy witnesses Jesus dispatched in Luke 10.

[244]Martin, *The Kingdom of the Cults*, 282

[245]Freeman, *The Story of Unity*, 105.

g. Radio (1922) and television (1969) and various educational outreaches were used to spread Unity teaching.

h. In 1920, fifty-eight acres were purchased in Jackson County, Missouri, which became the present site of Unity Village.

i. Myrtle Fillmore died in 1931; Charles married his secretary, Cora G. Dedrick, in 1933 and died in 1948.

j. Connie Fillmore Bazzy is the current president of USC.

II. Unity's Purpose and Philosophy

A. Unity's Purpose

1. Unity promises unlimited health, happiness, and prosperity to all who study its philosophy for living, "to help people realize their spiritual nature, so that they can apply spiritual principles to their daily experiences to live happy, healthy and more productive lives."

2. USC's and the Association of Unity Churches' (AUC) common goal "is to help people realize their divine potential" through publishing, education, and prayer.

B. Unity's Philosophy

1. Unity claims to be the *recovery* of the real truths of *primitive* Christianity.

2. It presents itself as a nonoffensive, nondenominational "school" of Christianity, to which any person "can subscribe to its teachings and still retain membership in any other church."[246]

3. Although it denies basic biblical doctrine, Unity insists that its metaphysical teaching crosses denominational lines. It teaches "that there is good in every religion and that we should keep our minds open so that we may find that good when the opportunity is presented."[247]

4. They claim no strict creed or dogma for subscription, but they consistently teach the system of belief that is described in the thirty articles of faith listed in *Unity's Statement of Faith*. They emphatically teach a basic metaphysical worldview that includes panentheism, monism, dualism, reincarnation, mysticism, the occult, and healing and wholeness through metaphysics.

C. Unity's Unique Teaching

1. USC is a mind science with an "open-ended" approach.

Unlike the other mind sciences, Unity's approach to "Truth" is open-ended. It encourages people to first secure a metaphysical worldview through Unity and then seek further mystical, psychic, and esoteric experiences through "prayer," meditation, and occultic mediums.

---

[246]Charles Fillmore, *The Adventure Called Unity* (Unity Village, Mo.: USC, n.d.), 6.
[247]Fillmore, *The Adventure Called Unity*, 6.

2. USC does not deny the existence of matter, as CS does.
   a. While the Fillmores denied the reality of evil, sickness, poverty, and death, they affirmed the reality of the material world. In USC, the material world is a manifestation of Spirit or Divine Mind; this Mind is expressed in matter as well as in mind or spirit.
   b. This theory, called panentheism, is the belief that God includes and permeates the material world, sometimes expressed as "the universe is God's Body."[248]
   c. USC does not teach directly the denial of medical treatment for the sick as CS does—although the Fillmores claimed that "prayer alone was enough to keep them whole."[249]
3. USC's belief in a Westernized form of reincarnation is not found in CS or RS.
   a. Reincarnation is "the belief that the soul or some power passes after death into another body."[250]
   b. After the death of the material body, the immaterial soul of man does not enter a final state but enters a cycle of rebirth.
   c. Reincarnation involves the notion of karma.
      (1) Karma literally means "doing, deeds, action, work."[251]
      (2) It represents one's deeds and the consequences of them, whether good or bad, and is a form of universal justice.
      (3) The state in which one is reincarnated is determined by the law of karma. Karmic debt will determine one's place in the future stages of the cycles of reincarnation.

III. Vital Statistics on Unity

A. *Membership*[252]
1. Unity estimates its membership at 90–110,000 with an additional 35,000 persons in more than 150 informal weekly study groups.
2. Unity has over 300 member churches worldwide, with an additional 610 ministries not yet chartered as churches.
3. There are 930 licensed and ordained Unity ministers and over 680 licensed Unity teachers.
4. Every month at least one new Unity study group is formed somewhere worldwide. (The closure rate is unknown.)

---

[248]See the discussion of panentheism in the section on Religious Science, Part II, Point II. A–C.
[249]Freeman, *The Story of Unity*, 156.
[250]Norman L. Geisler and J. Yutaka Amano, *The Reincarnation Sensation* (Wheaton, Ill.: Tyndale, 1986), 27.
[251]Geoffrey Parrinder, *Dictionary of Non-Christian Religions* (Philadelphia: Westminster Press, 1971), 286.
[252]The figures given below are as of April 1994, provided by AUC.

B. Literature Distribution

1. USC claims to reach over 6 million in 160 countries through its literature outreach.

2. Magazines include *Unity*, *Daily Word*, and *Wee Wisdom*, with a combined monthly circulation of more than 3 million.

3. USC publishes more than 80 metaphysical books, including *The Metaphysical Bible Dictionary*, which gives the metaphysical definition of common biblical words.

4. Mail

   a. USC distributes over 100 million pieces of mail annually in 13 foreign languages, including materials sent free by the "Silent-70" to orphanages, hospitals, prisons, and military bases.

   b. USC has been called the largest "mail-order religion" in the world, owing to its massive production of literature.[253]

   c. The over 100 million pieces of mail per year describe the benefits of Unity, available to those who will fill their minds with "happy thoughts," "kind ideas," and metaphysical affirmations.

5. Literature as missionaries

   Outreach through literature includes the publication of periodicals, books, and tapes in several languages—including Braille. In particular, the sophistically subtle and nonoffensive *Daily Word* is used as bait to lure people to become interested in Unity.

C. Other Ministries and Enterprises

1. USC headquarters is located on 1,400 acres near Lee's Summit, Missouri, in Unity Village, an incorporated municipality near Kansas City.

2. It operates a visitors' center (with guided tours), post office, bookstore, restaurant, gift shop, library, peace chapel, counseling center, a helpline for crisis counseling, and Sunday and Wednesday services.

3. The Silent Unity twenty-four-hour prayer ministry responds to more than 3 million people with an average of 7000 letters and 1,800 phone calls per day. It has branches in Great Britain, Australia, New Zealand, and the Netherlands.

4. Other outreaches include programs (such as "The Word" and "The Power of Your Potential") on more than 1000 radio and television stations, a leadership training school, educational classes, lectures, ministries, retreats, and local churches.

---

[253]Martin, *Kingdom of the Cults*, 279.

Part II: Theology

I. The Doctrine of Revelation and Scripture

A. Basic Statement of the Unity Position on Revelation and Scripture

1. All the sacred scriptures from the world's great religions can be used to discover truth.
2. All the sacred scriptures, including the Bible, must be interpreted metaphysically or allegorically, but not literally.
3. God spoke to the Fillmores so they could give the metaphysical understanding to interpret these sacred scriptures properly.
4. The Bible is helpful, but only to a limited degree.
5. Every person can receive revelations from God for oneself, within oneself.
6. Jesus was a master metaphysician who taught these Truths of Divine metaphysics.

B. Arguments Used by Unity to Support Its Position on Revelation and Scripture[254]

1. All the sacred scriptures from the world's great religions can be used to discover truth.

   a. "Spiritual principle is embodied in the sacred books of the world's living religions. Christians hold to the Bible as the supreme exponent of spiritual principle. They believe that the Bible is the greatest and most keenly spiritual of all scriptures, though they realize that other scriptures such as the Zend-Avesta and the Upanishads, as well as the teachings of Buddha, the Koran, and the Tao of Lao-tse and the writings of Confucius, contain expressions of eminent spiritual truths."[255]

   b. "We see good in all religions and we want everyone to feel free to find the Truth for himself wherever he may be led to find it."[256]

2. All the sacred scriptures, including the Bible must be interpreted metaphysically or allegorically, but not literally.

   a. USC is based on the Bible and other sacred writings, but metaphysically interpreted, not literally. USC is the "higher plane" of Christianity that helps us to understand properly their true metaphysical meaning.

---

[254]Note that arguments used by Unity are virtually the same as those used in Religious Science. See Part II, Point I.B under RS. Note that both Unity and Religious Science differ from Christian Science in their endorsement of the sacred scriptures of the world's religions.

[255]*What Unity Teaches*, USC, 4.

[256]*Modern Thought*, vol. 1 (1889), 42.

b. "We believe all the doctrines of Christianity spiritually [metaphysically] interpreted."[257]

c. "The New Testament is a veiled textbook for the initiate who is seeking degrees in the inner life. It gives rules for working out every mental state that may be found in the mind."[258]

d. "Our real aim [in presenting a metaphysical Bible dictionary] is to assist in leading the student into the inner or spiritual interpretation of the Bible, that he may apply it in the very best and most practical way in his own life. If one does not wish to accept our interpretations, but would rather do his own thinking, entirely apart from our suggestions, we fully recognize his right to do so."[259]

3. God spoke to the Fillmores so they could give the metaphysical understanding to interpret these sacred scriptures properly.

a. "The metaphysical interpretations given in this dictionary [i.e., the *Metaphysical Bible Dictionary*] are based on the practical teachings of Jesus Christ, as understood and taught by the Unity School of Christianity under the direction of Charles and Myrtle Fillmore, its founders."[260]

b. The Fillmores were "teachers, ministers, healers, builders. . . . about Charles Fillmore, there was something of the prophet . . . and he felt very strongly that God was speaking to him, using him to convey divine ideas. Like Joseph and Daniel he felt that God came to him in dreams and visions . . . and revealed to him much of the Truth about which he wrote and spoke."[261]

4. The Bible is helpful, but only to a limited degree.

a. "One of the greatest limitations to understanding the Bible is to insist on its infallibility."[262]

b. "We believe that the Scriptures are the testimonials of men who have in a measure apprehended the divine Logos but that their writings should not be taken as final."[263]

c. "Scripture may be a satisfactory authority for those who are not themselves in direct communion with the Lord."[264]

5. Every person can receive revelations from God for oneself, within oneself.

---

[257] Unity Statement of Faith, 6, #29.

[258] Preface, *Metaphysical Bible Dictionary* (Kansas City: USC, 1942). Hereafter referred to as *MBD*.

[259] *MBD*, preface.

[260] *MBD*, preface.

[261] Freeman, *The Story of Unity*, 16.

[262] Eric Butterworth, *Unity: A Quest for Truth* (n.p.: n.d.), 23.

[263] Unity Statement of Faith, 6, #27.

[264] *Unity Magazine*, 7, October 1896.

a. "We see good in all religions and we want everyone to feel free to find the Truth for himself wherever he may be led to find it."[265]

b. ". . . Truth is in every person, and it is only through the awakening of this inner Spirit that anyone can come to know Truth. . . . in the final analysis each individual has to find Truth for himself, within himself. It is this belief that is the basis of Charles Fillmore's teaching about the Bible."[266]

c. "When this peace is attained, the individual gets inspirations and revelations direct from infinite Mind."[267]

6. Jesus was a master metaphysician who taught these Truths of Divine metaphysics.

a. "The Master metaphysician said, 'That which is born of flesh is flesh; and that which is born of the Spirit is spirit.'"[268]

b. "Jesus, the man of Nazareth, demonstrated that this attainment [of the Christ self] is possible to man, and as a consequence He is the type-man."[269]

C. Refutation of Arguments Used by Unity to Support Its Position on Revelation and Scripture[270]

1. The Bible is complete and final; another "revelation" is not needed.

2. A metaphysical interpretation of the Bible is totally subjective, unverifiable, and therefore useless.

3. The God of the Bible does not accept all religions and therefore does not accept their so-called written revelations.

D. Arguments Used to Prove the Biblical Doctrine of Revelation and Scripture[271]

1. The Bible claims to be reliable and authoritative.

2. The Bible is complete and final.

3. Jesus and the New Testament writers consistently interpreted the Old Testament literally.

---

[265]Freeman, *The Story of Unity,* 42.

[266]Freeman, *The Story of Unity,* 186.

[267]Charles Fillmore, *Jesus Christ Heals* (Unity Village, Mo.: Unity School of Christianity, 1939), 82.

[268]*MBD,* 348.

[269]*MBD,* 345.

[270]Note that since the arguments used by Unity are virtually the same as those used in Religious Science, the refutations remain the same. See Part II, Point I.C under RS (cf. also the treatment under CS, Part II, Point I.C).

[271]Note that since the arguments used by Unity are virtually the same as those used in Religious Science and Christian Science, the biblical arguments against them remain the same. See Part II, Point I.D under RS and CS.

II. The Doctrine of God and the Trinity

A. The Unity Position on God Briefly Stated

1. God is impersonal Divine Mind, Principle, Law, Being, All Good.
2. Since God is All, then everything must be God.
3. Mind is All and therefore matter is the Body of God.[272]
4. God is the love in everybody and everything.
5. The Trinity represents a trinity of Being, not of persons.

B. Arguments Used by Unity to Support Its Position on God[273]

1. God is impersonal Divine Mind, Principle, Law, Being, All Good.

   a. "God is not a being or person having life, intelligence, love, power. God is that invisible, intangible, but very real, something we call life. God is perfect love and infinite power. God is the total of these, the total of all good, whether manifested or unexpressed."[274]

   b. "Belief in a personal God has retarded the spiritual progress of the race."[275]

   c. "Childlike, untrained minds say God is a personal being. The statement that God is principle chills them, and in terror they cry out, 'They have taken away my Lord, and I know not where they have laid him!' "[276]

2. Since God is All, then everything must be God.

   a. "God is all and all is God."[277] "God is Principle, Law, Being, Mind, Spirit, All Good."[278]

   b. "Each rock, tree, animal, everything visible, is a manifestation of the one Spirit—God—differing only in degree of manifestation; and each of the numberless modes of manifestation, or individualities, however insignificant, contains the whole."[279]

3. God is the love in everybody and everything.

   "God is not loving. God is love, the great heart of the universe and of man. . . . Yet God does not love anybody or anything. God is the love in everybody and everything. God is love; man becomes loving by permitting that which God is to find expression in word and act."[280]

---

[272]Note that this is a form of panentheism (see RS, Part II, Point II). This differs from Christian Science.

[273]Note that arguments used by Unity are virtually the same as those used in Christian Science. See Part II, Point II.B under CS.

[274]H. Emilie Cady, *Lessons in Truth* (Kansas City: Unity School of Christianity, 1941), 6.

[275]Sarah B. Scott, *The True Character of God* (Unity Village, Mo.: USC, n.d.), 3.

[276]Cady, *Lessons in Truth*, 10.

[277]*Unity Magazine*, August 1974, 40.

[278]*Unity Magazine*, 47, no. 5, 14.

[279]Cady, *Lessons in Truth*, 8.

[280]Fillmore, *Jesus Christ Heals*, 27.

4. The Trinity represents a trinity of Being, not of persons.

   a. "The Father is Principle. The Son is that Principle revealed in a creative plan. The Holy Spirit is the executive power of both Father and Son carrying out the creative plan."[281]

   b. "An idea arises in a man's mind of something that he wants to do; this idea is the Son. He expresses that idea in definite thought—that is the Spirit going forth to accomplish that whereto he has sent it."[282]

   c. "The Holy Ghost, or Holy Spirit, is the law of God in action."[283]

C. *Refutation of Arguments Used by Unity to Support Its Position on God*[284]

1. The God of the Bible is a personal being, not an impersonal Principle or "It."

2. Pantheism is false.

3. God is not the love in everybody and everything.

4. The God of the Bible is a triune personal being.

5. The Bible teaches that the Holy Spirit is the third person of the Holy Trinity.

D. *Arguments Used to Prove the Biblical Doctrine of God*[285]

1. The God of the Bible is personal.

2. The God of the Bible is triune.

3. God is separate from his creation.

4. The Holy Spirit is the third eternal person of the triune God.

III. The Person of Jesus Christ

A. *The Unity Position on the Person of Jesus Christ Briefly Stated*

1. The Christ is not the man Jesus, but the spiritual identity of Jesus, and is the true, spiritual, higher self of everyone.

2. Jesus was merely a human being who best demonstrated the Christ.

3. The mission of Jesus was to demonstrate the Christ, so that we too could follow him and take dominion over sin, sickness, disease, and death.

---

[281]*MBD*, 629.

[282]*MBD*, 629.

[283]*MBD*, 629.

[284]Note that since the arguments used by Unity are virtually the same as those used in Christian Science, the refutations remain the same. See Part II, Point II.C under CS.

[285]Note that since the arguments used by Unity are virtually the same as those used in Christian Science, the biblical arguments remain the same. See Part II, Point II.D under CS.

B. Arguments Used by Unity to Support Its Position on Jesus Christ[286]

1. The Christ is not the man Jesus, but the spiritual identity of Jesus, the true, spiritual, higher self of everyone.

   a. "Christ, meaning 'messiah' or 'anointed,' designates one who had received a spiritual quickening from God, while Jesus is the name of the personality. To the metaphysical Christian—that is, to him who studies the spiritual man—Christ is the name of the super-mind and Jesus is the name of the personal consciousness. The spiritual man is God's Son; the personal man is man's son."[287]

   b. "Jesus is the name that represents an individual expression of the Christ idea."[288]

   c. "By Christ is not meant the man Jesus."[289]

   d. "Christ is the divine-idea man. Christ is the only begotten Son of God, or the one complete idea of perfect man in Divine Mind. He is the embodiment of all divine ideas, such as intelligence, life, love, substance, and strength."[290]

   e. "This Christ, or perfect-man idea existing eternally in Divine Mind, is the true, spiritual, higher self of every individual. Each of us has within him the Christ, just as Jesus had, and we must look within to recognize and realize our sonship, our divine origin and birth, even as He did."[291]

2. Jesus was merely a human being who best demonstrated the Christ.

   a. Jesus was only a man, yet the only individual who has fully expressed the Christlike perfection which we all have the potential to achieve.

   b. "The difference between Jesus and us is not one of inherent spiritual capacity, but in difference of demonstration of it. Jesus was potentially perfect, we have not yet expressed it."[292]

3. The mission of Jesus was to demonstrate the Christ so that we too could follow him and take dominion over sin, sickness, disease, and death.

   a. "We believe that Jehovah God is incarnate in Jesus Christ and that all men may attain the Christ perfection by living the righteous life."[293]

[286]Note that arguments used by Unity are virtually the same as those used in Christian Science. See Part II, Point III.B under CS.

[287]Fillmore, *Jesus Christ Heals*, 10.

[288]*MBD*, 150–51.

[289]*Unity Magazine*, no. 2, 146.

[290]*MBD*, 150.

[291]*MBD*, 150.

[292]*What Unity Teaches*, Unity, 3.

[293]Unity's Statement of Faith, #26, 5.

b. "We believe that through conscious union with Jesus in the re-generation man can transform his body and make it perpetually healthy, therefore immortal, and that he can attain eternal life in this way and in no other way."[294]

C. *Refutation of Arguments Used by Unity to Support Its Position on Jesus Christ*[295]

1. Jesus is fully human, but he is also fully God (see point D).
2. Jesus is explicitly called the Christ many times.
3. Jesus himself claimed to be the Christ.
4. Many passages of Scripture show the Christ doing things that a "divine idea" could never do.
5. Jesus claimed to be much more than a Way-shower.

D. *Arguments Used to Prove the Biblical Doctrine of Jesus Christ*[296]

1. Jesus claimed to be God himself.
2. Jesus is called fully God in both the Old and New Testaments.
3. Jesus is described as fully man and fully God.
4. Jesus has the attributes and performs the actions of full deity (see Christian Science, Part II, Point II.D.2.c–d).
5. Jesus proved he is fully God by rising from the dead as he predicted (John 2:19).
6. Jesus is the Christ (see Christian Science, Part II, Point III.C.2).

IV. The Doctrine of Man

A. *The Unity Position on Man Briefly Stated*
1. Man is divine.
2. Man's body is a manifestation of Divine Mind.
3. Man is perfect, without sin; man does not sin because sin is unreal.
4. Each of us has the Christ within, just as Jesus had.

B. *Arguments Used by Unity to Support Its Position on Man*[297]

1. Man is divine.
    a. "It is the quickening of your divinity through the power of the Word. This divine nature is in us all, waiting to be brought into ex-

---

[294]Unity's Statement of Faith, #19, 4.

[295]Note that since the arguments used by Unity are virtually the same as those used in Christian Science, the refutations remain the same. See Part II, Point III.C under CS.

[296]Note that since the arguments used by Unity are virtually the same as those used in Christian Science, the biblical arguments against them remain the same. See Part II, Point III.D under CS.

[297]Note that arguments used by Unity are virtually the same as those used in Christian Science. See Part II, Point IV.B under CS.

pression through our recognition of the power and might of I AM."[298]

b. "Each of us is a unique, spiritual creation, a divine original with his or her own special God-given spark, capable of becoming a channel for God's love to pour into the world."[299]

2. Man's body is a manifestation of Divine Mind.

a. "We believe that the body of man is the highest-formed manifestation of creative Mind and that it is capable or unlimited expression of that Mind."[300]

b. "Man is the last and highest manifestation of divine energy, the fullest and most complete expression (or pressing out) of God. To man, therefore, is given dominion over all other manifestations."[301]

3. Man is perfect, without sin; man does not sin because sin is unreal.

a. "I am not a sinner. I never did sin. I cannot sin."[302]

b. "1. I deny that I have inherited disease, sickness, ignorance or any mental limitations whatsoever. 2. I deny that I am a child of the flesh. I deny all belief in evil, for God made all that really is and pronounced it good."[303]

c. "Never say, I don't know; I can't understand. Claim your Christ-understanding at all times and declare: I am not under any spell of human ignorance. I am one with the Infinite Understanding."[304]

d. "The difference between Jesus and us is not one of inherent spiritual capacity, but in difference of demonstration of it. Jesus was potentially perfect, we have not yet expressed it."[305]

C. *Refutation of Arguments Used by Unity to Support Its Position on Man*[306]

1. Man is a sinner in action and nature.

2. Finite man cannot be a part of an Infinite God.

D. *Arguments Used to Prove the Biblical Doctrine of Man*[307]

1. Man is a sinner and, apart from Jesus Christ, is separated from God.

2. Man is not divine in nature, nor is he part of God.

---

[298]*MBD*, 333.

[299]Fillmore, *The Adventure Called Unity*, 10.

[300]Unity's Statement of Faith, #18, 3.

[301]Cady, *Lessons in Truth*, #15, 9.

[302]*Unity Magazine*, 1936.

[303]Charles Fillmore, *Christian Healing* (Unity Village, Mo.: Unity School of Christianity, 1954).

[304]Fillmore, *Christian Healing*, 106–7.

[305]*What Unity Teaches*, Unity, 3.

[306]Note that since the arguments used by Unity are virtually the same as those used in Christian Science, the refutations remain the same. See Part II, Point IV.C under CS.

[307]Note that since the arguments used by Unity are virtually the same as those used in Christian Science, the biblical arguments remain the same. See Part II, Point IV.D under CS.

V. The Death and Resurrection of Jesus Christ

A. The Unity Position on the Death and Resurrection of Jesus Christ Briefly Stated

1. Death is unreal, so Jesus did not really die.

2. Since Jesus did not die, he could not be literally raised from the dead.

3. Jesus was raised from the dead spiritually and experienced Christ-consciousness.

4. Resurrection is the daily experience of those who are one with Christ-consciousness.

5. Unity writers disagree as to whether Jesus had to be reincarnated.

B. Arguments Used by Unity to Support Its Position on the Death and Resurrection of Jesus Christ

1. Death is unreal, so Jesus did not really die.

    a. "Physical death is not necessary. . . . Death has no place in the Absolute."[308]

    b. "The 'dead' in Scripture signifies those who are unconscious of Truth."[309]

    c. "At the crucifixion of Jesus it was the human consciousness of a perishable body that died."[310]

2. Since Jesus did not die, he could not be literally raised from the dead.

    a. "Resurrection. *Meta.* The raising of man's mind and body from sense to spiritual consciousness."[311]

    b. "Death does not change man and bring him into the resurrection and eternal life. Death has no place in the Absolute."[312]

    c. "Jesus resurrected the body that was crucified; this is forcibly brought out in the Scripture account of the crucifixion. He did this by putting into the body the true state of consciousness."[313]

3. Jesus was raised from the dead spiritually and experienced Christ-consciousness.

    a. "The resurrection is the lifting up of the whole man into the Christ-consciousness."[314]

    b. "At the crucifixion of Jesus it was the human consciousness of a perishable body that died"[315] (see also 2.C. above).

---

[308]*MBD*, 554.

[309]*MBD*, 167.

[310]*MBD*, 348.

[311]*MBD*, 553.

[312]*MBD*, 554.

[313]*MBD*, 349.

[314]*MBD*, 554.

[315]*MBD*, 348.

4. Resurrection is the daily experience of those who are one with Christ-consciousness.

a. "The resurrection is an organic change that takes place daily in all who are conforming their lives to the regenerating Truth of Jesus Christ. The resurrection takes place here and now in all who conform their lives to the spiritual law under which it works."[316]

b. "When man learns to live and apply the truth as did Jesus Christ, then the necessity for reincarnation will be done away with. He will have learned to live without dying."[317]

c. "We believe in the final resurrection of the body, through Christ. We do believe that we do free our minds and resurrect our bodies *by true thoughts and words* and that this resurrection is being carried forward *daily* and will be ultimate in a final purification of the body from all earthly errors."[318]

5. Unity writers disagree as to whether Jesus had to be reincarnated.

a. Jesus did not have to be reincarnated:

"Unity accepts reincarnation as a fact in human experience. We do not believe that it is necessary in the life and experience of Christ, the Son of God. In Christ there is no need for reincarnation, for in Christ there is no death. Death is a penalty for broken law. . . . Jesus broke no laws. When man learns to live and apply the truth as did Jesus Christ, then the necessity for reincarnation will be done away with. He will have learned to live without dying."[319]

b. Jesus was reincarnated:

"Jesus demands of the Pharisees, 'What think ye of Christ? whose son is he?' They answered, not as one might ordinarily expect, 'The son of Joseph,' but 'The son of David.' In other words, He was the reincarnation of David."[320]

C. Refutation of Arguments Used by Unity to Support Its Position on the Death and Resurrection of Jesus Christ[321]

1. The Bible teaches that Jesus did actually die physically on the cross (see point D).

2. The Bible clearly teaches that Jesus rose physically from the dead (see point D).

3. Reincarnation is refuted by the doctrine of resurrection taught in the Bible (see Point VII below).

---

[316]*MBD*, 554.

[317]Louis E. Meyer, *Reincarnation* (Unity Village, Mo.: Unity School of Christianity, 1976), 5.

[318]Unity's Statement of Faith, #28, 6, emphasis added.

[319]Meyer, *Reincarnation*, 4–5.

[320]Ernest C. Wilson, *Have We Lived Before?* (n.p., n.d.), 41.

[321]Note that since the arguments used by Unity are virtually the same as those used in Christian Science, the refutations remain the same. See Part II, Point V.C under CS.

> **D. Arguments for the Biblical Doctrine of the Death and Resurrection of Jesus Christ**[322]
>
> 1. Jesus did actually die.
> 2. The historical reality of the death and resurrection of Jesus forms essential twin truths of Christianity.

VI. The Doctrines of Sin and Salvation

A. The Unity Position on Sin and Salvation Briefly Stated

1. Sin, evil, disease, and death are unreal and an illusion. Sin is unreal, a destructive state of thought.
2. Heaven and hell are states of mind.
3. All will be saved.
4. Salvation comes when we choose to overcome our own ignorance by rejecting the idea of sin, sickness, death, or evil and believe only in good.
5. Everyone must save oneself; no one else can.
6. Jesus is merely our Way-shower to salvation.
7. Everyone passes through repeated incarnations until he reaches immortality through regeneration.[323]

B. Arguments Used by Unity to Support Its Position on Sin and Salvation

1. Sin, evil, disease, and death are unreal and an illusion. Sin is unreal, a destructive state of thought.

   a. "There is no evil (or devil). There is no reality or life or intelligence apart from Spirit. Pain, sickness, poverty, old age, and death are not real, and they have no power over me. There is nothing in the universe for me to fear."[324]

   b. "Man originally lived consciously in the spiritual part of himself. He fell by descending in his consciousness to the external or more material part of himself."[325]

2. Heaven and hell are states of mind.

   "Both [heaven and hell] are states of mind, and conditions, which people experience as a direct outworking of their thoughts, beliefs, words, and acts. If one's mental processes are out of harmony with the law of man's being, they result in trouble and sorrow; mental as well as bodily anguish overtakes one, and this is hell."[326]

---

[322]Note that since the arguments used by Unity are virtually the same as those used in Christian Science, the biblical arguments against them remain the same. See Part II, Point V.D under CS.

[323]This teaching differs both from CS and RS. See the discussion in Point VII below.

[324]Cady, *Lessons in Truth*, 35.

[325]Cady, *Lessons in Truth*, 14.

[326]*MBD*, 271.

3. All will be saved.

   a. "God's plan is ultimate salvation for every man."[327]

   b. "Unity tells us that the number and seriousness of our past mistakes do not matter to God. God holds no grudges and has no account book."[328]

4. Salvation comes when we choose to overcome our own ignorance by rejecting the idea of sin, sickness, death, or evil and believe only in good.

   a. "The inharmonies in the world can be eliminated by eliminating them from man's mind. This can be done by understanding that God's creation is all there is and knowing it to be good."[329]

   b. "Man's sins are forgiven when he ceases to sin and opens his mind to the fact that he is heir only to the good."[330]

   c. "The denial that the Fillmores taught is the denial of sorrow, the denial of limitations, the denial of sin, sickness, poverty, and death. They made of their teaching a joyous affirmation of life."[331]

5. Everyone must save oneself; no one else can.

"We have thought that we are to be saved by Jesus' making personal petitions and sacrifices for us, but now we see that we are to be saved by using the creative principles that he developed in Himself and that He is ever ready to co-operate with us in developing in ourselves by observing the law as He observed it. 'I in them, and thou in me, that they may be perfected into one.'"[332]

6. Jesus is merely our Way-shower to salvation.

   a. "We believe in Christ Jesus, the Son of God made manifest in Jesus of Nazareth, who overcame death, and who is now with us in His perfect body as the Way-Shower in regeneration for all men."[333]

   b. "Jesus showed man the way to gain atonement, or at-one-ment, with God, and He met and mastered every sin and weakness in order to reveal its utter powerlessness."[334]

7. Everyone passes through repeated incarnations until he reaches immortality through regeneration.

   a. "We believe that the dissolution of spirit, soul, and body, caused by death, is annulled by rebirth of the same spirit and soul in another body here on earth. We believe the repeated incarnations of man to

[327]Meyer, *Reincarnation*, 2.

[328]Fillmore, *The Adventure Called Unity*, 7.

[329]*MBD*, 158.

[330]*MBD*, 620.

[331]Freeman, *The Story of Unity*, 174.

[332]Fillmore, *Jesus Christ Heals*, 162.

[333]Unity's Statement of Faith, #3, 1.

[334]*The Way to Salvation* (N.p.: n.d.), 5.

be a merciful provision of our loving Father to the end that all may have opportunity to attain immortality through regeneration, as did Jesus."[335]

b. "Reincarnation replaces the old belief in condemnation and damnation by the faith of the everlasting mercy and forgiveness of God."[336]

c. "'The goal of man is eternal life, and in each incarnation that goal is brought nearer if Spirit is given an opportunity to express itself. When this is done, the true spiritual body will replace the physical body and all men will become like Jesus Christ.' Not reincarnation, but eternal life is the goal."[337]

C. *Refutation of Arguments Used by Unity to Support Its Position on Sin and Salvation*[338]

1. Sin, matter, evil, disease, and death are real.
2. The Bible does not teach universal salvation.
3. We cannot save ourselves; only Jesus Christ can.
4. Jesus is much more than a mere Way-shower.

D. *Arguments Used to Prove the Biblical Doctrine of Sin and Salvation*[339]

1. Sin is "missing the mark." It is anything that displeases God in thought, word, and deed.
2. Sin is universal and very real.
3. Sin has destructive results.
4. Sin requires payment that we cannot make for ourselves.
5. Jesus Christ paid the penalty for our sins.
6. Salvation is appropriated by trusting Christ's work of atonement.
7. Not all have salvation, and not all will be saved.

VII. Unity's Doctrine of Reincarnation

A. *The Unity Position on Reincarnation Briefly Stated*

1. After the death of the body, the soul falls asleep until our next incarnation.
2. The form we take in our successive rebirths is always that of another human being.

---

[335]Unity's Statement of Faith, Art. 22.

[336]Meyer, *Reincarnation,* 3.

[337]Meyer, *Reincarnation,* 8.

[338]Note that since the arguments used by Unity are virtually the same as those used in Christian Science, the refutations remain the same. See Part II, Point VI.C under CS.

[339]Note that since the arguments used by Unity are virtually the same as those used in Christian Science, the biblical arguments against them remain the same. See Part II, Point VI.D under CS.

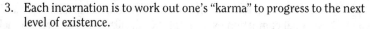

3. Each incarnation is to work out one's "karma" to progress to the next level of existence.

4. Unity writers disagree as to whether Jesus Christ needed to be reincarnated.

5. The goal of reincarnation is not continual reincarnations but eternal life.

B. Arguments Used by Unity to Support Its Position on Reincarnation

1. The Bible teaches reincarnation.[340]

   a. Malachi 4:5 and Matthew 11:14 teach that Malachi prophesied the reincarnation of the prophet Elijah, and it was fulfilled when John the Baptist appeared as a reincarnation of him (similar verses: Matt. 17:10–13; Mark 9:11–13; Luke 9:18–19).

   b. First Corinthians 15:53–54 underscores the repeated incarnations of man as a provision of our merciful God who will provide ultimate salvation for all through reincarnation: "For the perishable must clothe itself with the imperishable, and the mortal with immortality. When the perishable has been clothed with the imperishable, and the mortal with immortality, then the saying that is written will come true: 'Death has been swallowed up in victory.'"

   c. Galatians 6:7–8 refers to the unrelenting law of karma, which states that each person must pay for his good or bad actions, whether in this life or in future reincarnations: "Do not be deceived: God cannot be mocked. A man reaps what he sows. The one who sows to please his sinful nature, from that nature will reap destruction; the one who sows to please the Spirit, from the Spirit will reap eternal life" (cf. Matt. 26:52).

   d. In John 3:3 Jesus teaches the cycle of rebirth in reincarnation, wherein he tells Nicodemus that he must experience another rebirth to progress spiritually.

   e. In John 9:1–7 Jesus heals a man who was born blind because of the sins of his previous incarnations. This shows God's mercy in helping people work out their karma.

2. Reincarnation is a means of salvation.

   a. God is merciful and desires that none will perish, so he has provided reincarnation so that all will ultimately be saved.

   b. Our loving Father does not condemn or punish his children, for "God sent not his Son into the world to condemn the world; but that the world through him might be saved." Would you as a father want to punish your children continually, or help them to gain understanding of how to live without making mistakes? "Can your love be greater than the love of God?"[341]

---

[340]See Meyer, *Reincarnation,* for a discussion of some of these arguments.

[341]Meyer, *Reincarnation,* 3–4.

c. Reincarnation replaces the "old," incorrect belief in hell and eternal damnation by a wrathful God, with a God of love who helps all his children find eternal life.[342]

   d. The goal of reincarnation is not continual reincarnations, but rather spiritual improvement until ultimately we become like Jesus Christ and thereby gain eternal life. It provides repeated opportunities until we can learn to live like Jesus and then need reincarnation no longer.[343]

3. Reincarnation brings about justice and equality.

   a. Consider the problem of people "not born equal," such as those born poor, handicapped, or disadvantaged. Reincarnation becomes the great equalizer for all the inequalities of life.[344]

   b. It gives a just reason for suffering in this life—one that is based on the outworking of karma from past lives.

   c. It also rightly emphasizes personal responsibility for us and our own mistakes rather than blaming them on Adam or anyone else. This way we can "work out our *own* salvation" and satisfy justice ourselves.

   d. Reincarnation adequately explains why people such as Mozart and Shakespeare could have unique talents, skills, and genius in certain areas. This is due to the accumulation of achievements of hard-working souls through many incarnations.[345]

4. Many great religions teach reincarnation.

Reincarnation has been taught in the Eastern world for many centuries. It is newer to the West, but millions have believed in it since ancient history.

5. The evidence from past-life recalls show that some people remember experiences or feelings from previous incarnations.

Reincarnation explains the *déjà vu* experiences or feelings that we have all had of being somewhere or knowing someone before, when they otherwise appear to be new experiences to us.

6. Unity writers disagree as to whether Jesus Christ needed to be reincarnated (see the discussion at Point V.B.5 above).

C. Refutation of Arguments Used by Unity to Support Its Position on Reincarnation

1. Taken in context, the Bible verses used by Unity actually refute reincarnation rather than support it.

   a. John the Baptist (Mal. 4:5; Matt. 11:14)

---

[342]Meyer, *Reincarnation,* 3.

[343]Meyer, *Reincarnation,* 4–5.

[344]Meyer, *Reincarnation,* 2–8.

[345]Charles Fillmore, *The Twelve Powers of Man* (quoted in Meyer, *Reincarnation,* 5–6).

(1) John the Baptist was not a reincarnation of Elijah because in John 1:21 he said he was *not* Elijah.

(2) Luke 1:17 explains that John the Baptist would minister "in the spirit and power of Elijah," meaning with Elijah's function and authority, as a prophet, not as a reincarnation. John fulfilled the ministry Malachi had foretold (Mal. 4:5; Isa. 40:3).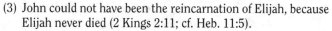

(3) John could not have been the reincarnation of Elijah, because Elijah never died (2 Kings 2:11; cf. Heb. 11:5).

(4) In Matthew 17, Elijah appears on the Mount of Transfiguration retaining the same identity; he does not appear as John.

b. 1 Corinthians 15

The whole chapter teaches on resurrection; Paul mentions resurrection nineteen times, but never reincarnation.

c. Galatians 6:7–8

(1) Nowhere does Galatians 6:7–8 mention or teach karma or reincarnation. In context it does speak of the equal, impartial judgment of God on all people.

(2) "Sowing to the Spirit" is a metaphor for saving faith in Christ (Rom. 5:1–11).

(3) Those who are righteous through Christ will gain eternal life, and the unrighteous, who "sow to their sinful nature," will reap eternal judgment (Matt. 25:41, 46).

d. John 3:3

(1) John 3:3 speaks of being born-again, not of reincarnation.

(2) In the context, Jesus describes being born-again as a spiritual rebirth, not a cycle of endless physical rebirths.

(3) Jesus is telling Nicodemus that *physical* birth cannot give *spiritual* life (vv. 4–6) and that our foremost need is to receive new spiritual life *from the Spirit of God* (vv. 5–6, 8). Physical rebirth (like reincarnation) cannot lead to spiritual life, as Nicodemus mistakenly thought (v. 4).

(4) Verse 6 says, "Spirit gives birth to spirit," meaning it is the Spirit of God who gives birth to our spirit so that we can have fellowship with him; we cannot gain it through our own efforts.

(5) "Born-again" in Greek may also mean "born from above" (as it does every time it is used in John—3:31; 19:11). It is equated with *born of the Spirit* (vv. 5–6, 8), a spiritual birth given to a soul that is dead because of sin (Eph. 2:2).

(6) If Jesus were teaching reincarnation here, it would contradict what he said in many other places. For example, reincarnation contradicts what Jesus said about the eternal resurrection of the just and the unjust (Matt. 24:41, 46). It also is at odds with

what he said to the criminal on the cross: "I tell you the truth, today you will be with me in paradise" (Luke 23:43).

e. John 9:3

John 9:3 actually refutes reincarnation because Jesus emphatically states that the man was *not* born blind because of his sin, or his parents' sin, but rather "so that the work of God might be displayed in his life." Had Jesus believed in the law of karma, we would have expected him to say that the man *was* born blind because of sin in a previous life.

2. God has provided salvation through atonement, not reincarnation.

a. While the Bible certainly affirms the love and mercy of God, it also clearly teaches that he provided a once-and-for-all solution for sin through Christ's unique atonement (Heb. 7:27; 9:12, 28; 10:10). This was God's method to help people find forgiveness of sin and reconciliation with him.

b. In Christianity, God's love is seen in a much greater fashion than in reincarnation, as he himself comes in the flesh to pay the penalty for sin that sinful people could never pay for themselves (Eph. 2:8–9; Rom. 3–4).

(1) The love of God cannot be understood apart from his justice and holiness, so whenever we deal with the real love of God, the atonement of Christ is always an integral part of it.

(2) In the Bible, God's love and sacrificial atonement are always tied together (John 3:16; Rom. 5:8), because it was the sacrifice of his Son that manifested his love.

3. The Bible teaches that hell and eternal punishment are real.

a. The biblical doctrine of hell and eternal punishment does not need to be replaced. It is a part of the total revelation of Scripture. Jesus spoke a great deal about the reality of hell. (See Christian Science, Part II, Point VI.D.7.)

b. Ultimately there are some who will reject the offer of salvation (Matt. 7:13–14, 21–23; 25:41, 46; 2 Thess. 1:8–9; Rev. 19:20–21; 20:11–15).

4. Reincarnation does not solve the problem of evil.

a. Reincarnation simply ignores the problem of evil by moving it back to previous lives; it does not come closer to explaining the presence of evil or its origin.[346]

b. There is no proof that suffering or inequalities are caused by the sins of previous incarnations.

(1) The Sovereign God of the Bible works out all the "inequalities" (as viewed from a human perspective) in the wisdom of his

---

[346]Norman Geisler, *When Skeptics Ask* (Wheaton, Ill.: Victor Books, 1990), 241ff.

eternal plan of redemption. "Making things equal" is the Creator's role rather than leaving it up to the finite creation to reconcile (Rev. 21:4).

(2) Romans 5:12 tell us that sin is in the world because of Adam's transgression, not because of sins of a previous lifetime.

(3) Human history amply demonstrates the total failure of mankind to improve its fallen state, make up these inequalities, and progress spiritually. One would have seen greater moral and spiritual progress by now if reincarnation were true.

5. Other religions teach reincarnation, but this does not confirm it as true.

a. Other religions of antiquity also taught polytheism and human sacrifice. So is Unity wrong for not believing in these things?

b. The reliable test for truth is not the popularity of a teaching, but its agreement with the revelation of the Bible, which alone has credentials to support its truth-claims.

6. Past-life recalls or *déjà vu* experiences do not prove reincarnation.

a. *Déjà vu* experiences do not prove reincarnation because they are solely subjective evaluations that cannot be verified.

b. Why do people not remember their previous incarnations to learn from their mistakes if reincarnation is true?

c. So-called past-life recalls can be used by Satan to supernaturally deceive people into believing that reincarnation takes place and to dupe them into believing that Unity is true and historic Christianity is not (Ex. 7:8–13; Matt. 7:15, 21–23; 2 Thess. 2:7–12).

7. Reincarnation is ultimately antihumanitarian.

a. People in places like India, who believe in karma, do not help those who suffer because they are afraid it will interfere with the victim's working out his or her own salvation. Such help may cause the sufferers to come back to endure greater hardship because they did not pay off their karmic debt in this life.

b. A good Samaritan could actually alter his own karma through the "sin" of interfering with someone else's karmic debt. Yet, if he refuses to act to help, he still commits evil by doing nothing![347] Thus the reincarnationist is caught in an illogical situation.

---

[347]Geisler and Amano, *The Reincarnation Sensation*, 109.

Section 4:
Witnessing Tips

I. The Mind Sciences and the Problem of "Term-Twisting"

A. Beware of "Term-Twisting"

In this practice people use biblical or Christian terms (such as *God, Jesus, salvation, atonement, resurrection, Christ*) but fill them with different, unbiblical, metaphysical meanings (2 Peter 2:1–3). Ask them to define their terms.

B. Study Key Words

Study the key biblical words in the glossaries of *Science and Health* (579 ff.), *The Science of Mind* (575 ff.), and *The Metaphysical Bible Dictionary*, and become acquainted with their metaphysical meanings. Be prepared to give the corresponding definitions from the Bible. This is essential to communicating effectively with a mind scientist.

C. Be Alert to Selective Use of Scripture

Be alert to the way mind scientists twist the Scriptures in their interpretation by "spiritualizing" Bible passages—taking them out of context and then reading into the text a metaphysical, "higher" truth. The mind sciences also tend to ignore passages that do not support their theology on a given subject.

II. Specific Approaches and Methods for Witnessing to a Mind Scientist

A. The Gnosticism Approach

1. You may ask, "Were you aware that teachings much like your leader's were promoted centuries ago by ancient teachers who claimed a superior form of 'spiritual knowledge,' and these teachings were rejected by the historic Christian Church?"

2. Although the modern mind sciences do not teach ancient Gnosticism per se, the parallels are nevertheless so close that one can adequately demonstrate that the mind sciences are a present-day revival and clever repackaging of these historical false teachings.

3. Ask the mind scientist if he or she would like to do a Bible study with you in the epistle of 1 John. This book is full of refutations of basic mind science theology.

B. The Worldview Challenge

1. The leaders of the mind sciences superimpose a metaphysical worldview on the Bible, thereby implying that the God of the Bible cannot adequately speak to the human race for himself. They claim that only through their metaphysical system can someone really know God and his truth.

2. The challenge to the mind scientists is to ask them: "What gives their leader (or themselves) the right to superimpose this metaphysical interpretative grid over the Scriptures?" For the mind scientists simply to claim a higher authority in their leader does not legitimize their claim.

   a. Example: It is not enough proof for a Christian Scientist simply to reiterate Eddy's bold claim that "she is equal to Jesus Christ, a fulfillment of Bible prophecy of the woman of Revelation 12, the God-chosen revelator for this age,[348] with a superior and final revelation to all that has gone before."[349] There must be objective proof for these incredible assertions.

   b. We must ask for her credentials and objective evidence that proves she has the authority to make such audacious claims. For us to accept the mind science view we must believe that Mary Baker Eddy, Ernest Holmes, or the Fillmores have authority above Jesus Christ and the Bible.

C. The Plagiarism Approach (in Christian Science only)

This approach is only for people who are open-minded enough to honestly examine these examples of Eddy's plagiarism:[350]

1. Of P. P. Quimby's *Science of Man*, shown in the *New York Times*, July 10, 1904.

2. Of "The English Reader," by Lindley Murray, 4th ed., Pittsburgh, 1823.

3. Possibly of Francis Lieber, "The Metaphysical Religion of Hegel."

D. The Weakness-Strength Approach

1. Contrast the richness of the personal God of the Bible with the impersonal Principle of the mind sciences. A personal God with whom one can have a relationship is infinitely more satisfying than an impersonal force that cannot relate to anyone or anything.

---

[348]Mary Baker Eddy, *The First Church of Christ Scientist and Miscellany* (Boston: CS Publishing Society, 1913), vii.

[349]*Mrs. Eddy's Place* (Boston: CS Publishing Society, 1943).

[350]Cited in Walter R. Martin, *Kingdom of the Cults* (Minneapolis: Bethany House, 1985), 128, 130, 130–31 respectively.

2. Contrast the weakness of the metaphysical interpretation of the Bible versus the strength of evidence that confirms the normal, literal interpretive method.

   a. The metaphysical approach is too subjective to be of any value. What if someone's subjective experience is wrong?

   b. The Bible's message is built on objective, historical, verifiable facts.

3. The mind sciences do not adequately deal with the problem of sin, sickness, suffering, and evil.

   a. They redefine these entities and then try to deny their existence or power over mankind. This is not a practical help in assisting people to overcome these real entities.

   b. In contrast, one strength of Christianity is that it offers mankind a personal Savior who comes and lives within us to empower us to have victory over sin, sickness, suffering, and evil. He also can empathize and help us in our pain because he has shared in our humanity and experienced it for himself (Heb. 2:14–18).

4. Contrast the weakness of reincarnation (in Unity School only) with the biblical teaching of resurrection.

   a. Reincarnation is a wicked, merciless system that inflicts punishment on those who are destined to repeat the sins of their past lives because they do not know what they were. It produces fatalism, pessimism, and despair.

   b. It comes from Hinduism, and the devastating results of this belief can be seen in the social horror of the cultures where it is widespread, such as India.[351]

---

[351]See Robert A. Morey, *Reincarnation and Christianity* (Minneapolis: Bethany, 1980), 43–44. Morey states more than twenty reasons for the inadequacies of the theory of reincarnation.

Section 5: Bibliography

Part I: General Sources on the Mind Sciences

Ankerberg, John and John Weldon. *The Facts on the Mind Sciences.* Eugene, Ore.: Harvest House, 1993.

Concise question-and-answer format on CS, RS, USC, Divine Science, New Thought, and Silva Mind Control.

Ehrenborg, Todd B. *Speaking the Truth in Love to the Mind Sciences.* 1990. Christian Research Institute, P.O. Box 500, San Juan Capistrano, Calif. 92693.

A practical tool for evangelism that covers the background and theology of CS, RS, USC, and contrasts biblical refutations to them on the same page, along with guidelines for witnessing.

Harm, Frederick R. *How to Respond to the Science Religions.* St. Louis: Concordia, 1981.

Short, concise chapters on CS, RS, USC, New Thought, and Divine Science.

Hoekema, Anthony A. *The Four Major Cults.* Grand Rapids: Eerdmans, 1963.

An older but solid treatment of CS.

Martin, Walter R. *The Kingdom of the Cults.* Minneapolis: Bethany House, 1985.

Classic work on the cults that contains an excellent analysis of CS and USC with documentation of Eddy's plagiarisms.

Part II: Selected Bibliography (Christian Science)

I. Primary Sources on Christian Science (CS)[352]

Science and Health with Key to the Scriptures.

Eddy's highest authoritative work in CS, and the most used; considered one of the "Pastors" of the CS Church, along with the Bible.

---

[352]All primary sources listed here are published in Boston by the Christian Science Publishing Society or by Trustees under the will of Mary Baker Eddy.

Manual of the Mother Church. 1895.

Contains rules and bylaws that ensure Eddy's authoritarian hold on the church even after her death.

Miscellaneous Writings. 1896.

Eddy's addresses, letters, sermons, poems, and teachings on various subjects; originally from the *CS Journal.*

Retrospection and Introspection. 1891.

Eddy's own account of her early life and the steps leading to the "discovery" of CS.

Rudimental Divine Science. 1891.

Eddy provides questions and answers on the teachings of CS.

No and Yes. 1891.

Eddy's defense of CS in a question-and-answer format to correct what she claims are common misconceptions about it.

Christian Science Versus Pantheism. 1898.

Eddy's unsuccessful attempt to separate her system from pagan pantheism.

Christ and Christmas. 1907.

In picture and poem, Mary Baker Eddy sees herself as equal to and the successor of Jesus Christ.

A Century of Christian Science Healing. 1966.

An experiential apologetic that describes the so-called healing of Eddy that led to the founding of her church and includes stories of healings in CS since that time, and articles on the CS perspective of healing.

Other works by Eddy include *Unity of Good*; *Pulpit and Press*; *Christian Healing*; *The People's Idea of God*; *The First Church of Christ, Scientist, and Miscellany*.

II. Secondary Sources on Christian Science

Dakin, Edwin. *Mrs. Eddy.* New York: Charles Scribner's Sons, 1929.

An excellent in-depth and revealing biography that gives important historical background exposing the myths around Eddy.

Dresser, Horatio W., ed. *The Quimby Manuscripts.* New York: Thomas Y. Crowell, 1921.

Although not written from a biblical perspective, the first edition contains the letters which Eddy (at that time Mrs. Patterson) addressed to Dr. P. P. Quimby. This book demonstrates the connection between P. P. Quimby's original ideas and Eddy's later use of them.

Haushalter, Walter M. *Mrs. Eddy Purloins From Hegel.* Boston: A. A. Beauchamp, 1936.

This reveals the contents of a manuscript reportedly written by Francis Lieber on "The Metaphysical Religion of Hegel" and appears to show how Eddy plagiarized from it.

Martin, Walter R. *Christian Science*. Minneapolis: Bethany House, 1974.

A good, brief introductory booklet.

Martin, Walter R. and Norman H. Klann. *The Christian Science Myth*. Grand Rapids: Zondervan, 1955.

This out-of-print text is the best and most thorough theological and philosophical treatment available from a Christian perspective. Some Christian college or seminary libraries may have copies.

Milmine, Georgine. *The Life of Mary Baker G. Eddy and the History of Christian Science*. New York: Doubleday, 1909. Reprint: Grand Rapids: Baker, 1971.

This is the best, most detailed, unbiased historical account. The author, who was a *McClure's Magazine* writer and a contemporary of Eddy, reveals much damaging information that the Mother Church has tried to suppress.

Part III: Selected Bibliography (Religious Science)

I. Primary Sources on Religious Science

Armor, Reginald. *Ernest Holmes: The Man*. Los Angeles: Science of Mind Publications, 1977.

Informal reminiscences about Holmes by a colleague of over forty years.

Holmes, Ernest. *The Science of Mind*. New York: Dodd, Mead, 1965.

The primary authoritative textbook of RS; 667 pages.

____. *What Religious Science Teaches*. Los Angeles: Science of Mind Publications, 1974.

A 93-page summary booklet of RS teaching.

Other topical booklets by Holmes of less than a hundred pages each include *Ideas for Living; Know Yourself! Freedom to Live; It's Up to You! Thoughts Are Things; Ten Ideas That Make a Difference; Freedom From Stress; Living Without Fear; Discover a Richer Life; The Magic of the Mind; It Can Happen To You; Practical Application of Science of Mind; The Basic Ideas of Science of Mind; Journey Into Life; Observations; Spiritual Awareness*.

II. Secondary Sources on Religious Science

See books above in the "General Sources on the Mind Sciences" section that have chapters on Religious Science.

Part IV: Selected Bibliography (Unity School of Christianity)

I. Primary Sources on Unity School of Christianity

The Unity literature list has more than a hundred titles from various metaphysical writers. A few of the more important works are given below.

Cady, H. Emilie. *Lessons in Truth*. Kansas City: Unity School of Christianity (USC), 1941.

The first Unity book, published in 1889, and its basic textbook of 12 lessons on metaphysical Christianity explaining the basic principles of Unity, including lists of denials and affirmations.

____. *God Is a Present Help*. Unity Village, Mo.: USC, 1942.

Fillmore, Charles. *Jesus Christ Heals*. Unity Village, Mo.: USC, 1939.

____. *Christian Healing*. Unity Village, Mo.: USC, 1954.

Teaching on metaphysical healing.

____. *The Twelve Powers of Man*. Unity Village, Mo.: USC, 1943.

The supposed twelve spiritual centers in the body on which one can concentrate to release spiritual forces.

____. *What Practical Christianity Stands For*. Unity Village, Mo.: USC, 1939.

____. *Dynamics for Living*. Unity Village, Mo.: USC, 1967.

A compilation of the core of his teachings.

____. *The Revealing Word*. Unity Village, Mo.: USC, 1959.

Metaphysical definitions of 1,200 words and phrases.

Freeman, James D. *The Story of Unity*. Lee's Summit, Mo.: USC, 1954.

The history of the Unity movement, written in 1951 and updated in 1978.

____. *The Case for Reincarnation*. Unity Village, Mo.: USC, 1986.

Metaphysical Bible Dictionary. Kansas City: USC, 1942.

A 709-page encyclopedia giving the metaphysical interpretation of Bible words and names.

II. Secondary Sources on Unity School of Christianity

See books above in the "General Sources on the Mind Sciences" section that have chapters on Unity School of Christianity.

Miller, Elliot. "Unity School of Christianity." In *Walter Martin's Cults Reference Bible*. Santa Ana, Calif.: Vision House, 1981.

A thorough article on USC. This Bible has excellent Christian responses to many biblical texts twisted by the mind sciences on the pages where the passages appear.

III. Sources Evaluating Reincarnation

Albrecht, Mark. *Reincarnation: A Christian Appraisal*. Downers Grove, Ill.: InterVarsity Press, 1982.

Geisler, Norman L., and J. Yutaka Amano, *The Reincarnation Sensation*. Wheaton: Tyndale, 1986.

Excellent analysis of altered states, past-life recall, Eastern mysticism, and other popular New Age and reincarnation philosophies.

Martin, Walter R. *The Riddle of Reincarnation*. Santa Ana, Calif.: Vision House, 1977.

A good, brief introductory booklet.

Morey, Robert A. *Reincarnation and Christianity*. Minneapolis: Bethany House, 1980.

Snyder, John. *Reincarnation vs. Resurrection*. Chicago: Moody Press, 1984.

Section 6:
Parallel Comparison Chart

Mind Sciences	The Bible

God

[CS] "The Scriptures imply that God is All-in-all. From this it follows that nothing possesses reality nor existence except the divine Mind and His ideas" (*S/H*, 331).

[RS] "The whole universe is the manifestation of a Unity which men call God" (*What Religious Science Teaches*, 12).

[USC] "Each rock, tree, animal, everything visible, is a manifestation of the one Spirit—God—differing only in degree of manifestation; and each of the numberless modes of manifestation, or individualities, however insignificant, contains the whole" (Cady, *Lessons in Truth*, 8).

[RS] "God is not a person, God is a Presence personified in us" (*S/M*, 308).

[USC] "The Father is Principle. The Son is that Principle revealed in the creative plan. The Holy Spirit is the executive power of both Father and Son carrying out the creative plan" (*MBD*, 629).

[USC] "God is not a being or person, having life, intelligence, love, power. God is perfect love and infinite power. God is the total of these, the total of all good" (*Lessons in Truth*, 6).

"In the beginning you laid the foundations of the earth, and the heavens are the *work of your hands*. They will *perish*, but you remain; they will all wear out like a garment" (Ps. 102:25–26).* [God is distinct from his creation.]

"It is I who *made the earth* and *created mankind upon it*. My own hands *stretched out* the heavens; I marshaled their starry hosts" (Isa. 45:12). [God is distinct from his creation.]

"They exchanged the truth of God for a lie, and worshiped and served created things rather than the Creator" (Rom. 1:25).

"But the Egyptians are men and *not God*; their horses are *flesh and not spirit*" (Isa. 31:3).

"God is in heaven and you are on earth" (Eccl. 5:2).

"And a voice from heaven said, 'This is my Son, whom I love; with him I am well pleased.'" (Matt 3:17). [This shows a personal subject-object relationship.]

---

*Italics in the text of either column in this parallel comparison chart have been added for emphasis and are not in the original works cited.

[CS] "Man originated not from dust, materially, but from Spirit, spiritually" (*Misc. Writ.*, 57). "Man is not matter; he is not made up of brain, blood, bones, and other material elements.... Man is spiritual and perfect.... Man is idea, the image, of Love; he is not physique" (*S/H*, 475).

[RS] "There is that within *every* individual which partakes of the nature of the Universal Wholeness and—in so far as it operates *is God*. That is the meaning of Immanuel, the meaning of the word Christ. There is that within us which partakes of the nature of the Divine Being, and since it partakes of the nature of the Divine Being, we are divine" (*S/M*, 33–34).

[USC] "So we say that each individual manifestation of God contains the whole; not for a moment meaning that each individual is God in His entirety, so to speak, but that each is God come forth, shall I say? in different quantity or degree" (Cady, *Lessons in Truth*, 9).

"The LORD God formed man from the dust of the ground and breathed into his nostrils the breath of life, and man became a living being" (Gen. 2:7).

"Know that the LORD is God. It is he who has made us, and we are his; we are his people, the sheep of his pasture" (Ps. 100:3).

"God is not a man, that he should lie, nor a son of man, that he should change his mind" (Num. 23:19).

"When the crowd saw what Paul had done, they shouted, ... 'The gods have come down to us in human form!' But when the apostles Barnabas and Paul heard of this, they tore their clothes and rushed out into the crowd, shouting: 'Men, why are you doing this? *We too are only men, human like you.* We are bringing you good news, telling you to turn from these worthless things *to the living God, who made heaven and earth and sea and everything in them*" (Acts 14:11, 14–15).

Jesus Christ

[CS] "The Christian who believes in the First Commandment is a monotheist. Thus he virtually unites with the Jew's belief in one God, and recognizes that *Jesus Christ is not God*, as Jesus himself declared, but is the Son of God" (*S/H*, 361).

[RS] "Jesus never thought of himself as different from others" (*S/M*, 361). "Mental Science does not deny the divinity of Jesus; but it does affirm the divinity of all people.

"You are from *below*, I am from *above*; you are of *this world*, I am *not of this world*. I said therefore to you, that you shall die in your sins; for unless you believe that *I am He*, you shall die in your sins.... Truly, truly, I say to you, before Abraham was born, I am'" (John 8:23–24, 58 [NASB]). [Jesus takes the divine name of *I am* (YHWH, Jehovah) from Exodus 3:14 for himself.]

91

It does not deny that Jesus was the son of God; but it affirms that all men are the sons of God" (*S/M*, 161–62).

[USC] "The difference between Jesus and us is not one of inherent spiritual capacity, but in difference of demonstration of it. Jesus was potentially perfect, and He expressed that perfection; we are potentially perfect, and we have not yet expressed it" (*What Unity Teaches*, 3).

[CS] "Jesus is the human man, and Christ is the divine idea; hence the duality of Jesus the Christ" (*S/H*, 473).

[RS] "JESUS—the name of a man. Distinguished from the Christ. . . . Christ is not limited to any person, nor does He appear in only one age" (*S/M*, 603, 363).

[USC] "By Christ is not meant the man Jesus" (*Unity Magazine*, no. 2, p. 146).

"'*I and the Father are one.*' Again the Jews picked up stones to stone him, but Jesus said to them, 'I have shown you many great miracles from the Father. For which of these do you stone me?' 'We are not stoning you for any of these,' replied the Jews, 'but for blasphemy, because you, a mere man, *claim to be God*'" (John 10:30–33; cf. 5:18).

"For in Christ all the fullness of the Deity lives in bodily form" (Col. 2:9).

"'Are you the Christ, the Son of the Blessed One?' *I am,*' said Jesus" (Mark 14:61–62).

"'Who do you say that I am?' Simon Peter answered, '*You are the Christ*, the Son of the Living God.' Jesus replied, 'Blessed are you Simon son of Jonah, for this was *not revealed to you by man, but by my Father in heaven*'" (Matt. 16:15–17).

Death and Resurrection

[CS] "Jesus' students, not sufficiently advanced fully to understand their Master's triumph, did not perform many wonderful works, until they saw him after his crucifixion and learned that he had *not died*" (*S/H*, 45–46). "RESURRECTION. Spiritualization of thought; a new and higher idea of immortality, or spiritual existence; material belief yielding to spiritual understanding" (*S/H*, 593).

"Jesus called out with a loud voice, 'Father, into your hands I commit my spirit.' When he had said this, he breathed his last" (Luke 23:46).

"But when they came to Jesus and found that he was already dead, they did not break his legs" (John 19:33).

"He humbled himself and became obedient to death—even death on a cross!" (Phil 2:8).

[RS] "The resurrection is the death of the belief that we are separated from God. For death is to the illusion alone and not to Reality. God did not die. What happened was that man awoke to Life. The awakening must be on the part of man since God already is Life" (*S/M*, 413).

[USC] "We believe that we do free our minds and resurrect our bodies by true thoughts and words and that this resurrection is being carried forward daily and will ultimate in a final purification of the body from all earthly errors. Through this process we shall be raised to the consciousness of continuous health and eternal life here and now, following Jesus Christ in the regeneration or 'new birth'" (*Unity's Statement of Faith*, Art. 28).

"And if the Spirit of him who raised Jesus from the dead is living in you, he who raised Christ from the dead will also give life to your mortal bodies through his Spirit, who lives in you" (Rom. 8:11).

"And if *Christ has not been raised*, our preaching is useless and so is your faith. More than that, we are then found to be false witnesses about God, for we have testified about God that he *raised Christ from the dead*. And if Christ has not been *raised*, your faith is futile; you are *still in your sins*" (1 Cor. 15:14–15, 17).

"Jesus answered them, 'Destroy this temple, and I will raise it again in three days.' But the temple he had spoken of was his *body*" (John 2:19, 21). [Body = Greek: *soma* = physical body.]

Sin

[CS] "In Science there is no fallen state of being; for therein is no inverted image of God, no escape from the focal radiation of the Infinite" (*No and Yes*, p. 17). "Christ came to destroy the belief of sin" (*S/H*, 473). "The way to escape the misery of sin is to cease sinning. There is no other way" (*S/H*, 327).

[RS] "SIN—We have tried to show that there is no sin but a mistake, and no punishment but a consequence. The Law of cause and effect. Sin is merely missing the mark. God does not punish sin. As we correct our mistakes, we forgive our own sins" (*S/M*, 633).

[USC] "The 'eternal sin,' or unpardonable sin, . . . is the belief that

"Therefore, just as *sin entered* the world through one man, and death through sin, and in this way *death came to all men*, because *all sinned*—for before the law was given, sin was in the world" (Rom. 5:12–13).

"Christ Jesus came into the world to save sinners—of whom I am the worst" (1 Tim. 1:15).

"If we claim to be without sin, we *deceive* ourselves and the truth is not in us. *If we confess our sins*, he is faithful and just to forgive us our sins and purify us from all unrighteousness, *If we claim we have not sinned*, we make him out to be a *liar* and his word has no place in our lives" (1 John 1:8–10).

God is the creator of disease or in-harmony of any nature. . . . Man's sins are forgiven when he ceases to sin and opens his mind to the fact that he is heir only to the good" (*MBD*, 620).

[USC] "The inharmonies in the world can be eliminated by elimi-nating them from man's mind. This can be done by understanding that God's creation is all that there is and knowing it to be good" (*MBD*, 158).

"Yet he [the Lord] does not leave the guilty unpunished" (Ex. 34:7).

"*Everything* that does not come from faith is *sin*" (Rom. 14:23).

"Everyone who sins breaks the law; in fact, sin is lawlessness" (1 John 3:4).

"The wages of sin is death" (Rom. 6:23).

Salvation

[CS] "Salvation—Life, Truth, and Love understood and demon-strated as supreme over all; sin, sickness, and death destroyed" (*S/H*, 593). "This salvation means: Saved from error, or error overcome" (*Misc. Writ.*, 89). "Final deliverance from error, whereby we rejoice in immortality, boundless freedom, and sinless sense, is not reached through paths of flowers nor by pin-ning one's faith without works to another's vicarious effort" (*S/H*, 22). "Man as God's idea is already saved with an everlasting salvation" (*Misc. Writ.*, 261).

[RS] "SALVATION—is not a thing, not an end, but a Way. The Way of Salvation is through man's unity with the Whole. Grace is the givingness of Spirit to Its Creation" (*S/M*, 631).

"We believe that the ultimate goal of life to be a complete emanci-pation from all discord of every na-ture, and that this goal is sure to be attained by all" (*What RS Teaches*, 50).

"Since we have now been justi-fied *by his blood*, how much more shall we be saved from God's wrath through him! For if, when *we were God's enemies*, we were *reconciled to him through the death of his Son*, how much more, having been reconciled, shall we be saved through his life!" (Rom. 5:9–10).

"He himself *bore our sins* in *his body* on the tree, so that we might die to sins and live for righteous-ness; *by his wounds* you have been healed" (1 Peter 2:24; cf. Isa. 53:4–12).

"*Believe* in the Lord Jesus, and *you will* be saved" (Acts 16:31).

"If you confess with your mouth, '*Jesus is Lord*,' and *believe in your heart* that God raised him from the *dead*, you will be saved" (Rom. 10:9).

"For it is *by grace* you have been saved, *through faith*—and this *not from yourselves*, it is the *gift* of God—*not of works*, so that no one can boast" (Eph. 2:8–9, cf. Titus 3:5–7).

[USC] "Being 'born-again' or 'born from above' is not a miraculous change that takes place in man; it is the establishment of that which has always existed as the perfect man idea of divine Mind" (*Christian Healing*, 24).

"I tell you the truth, *unless* a man is born of water and the Spirit, he cannot enter the kingdom of God. Flesh gives birth to flesh, but the Spirit gives birth to spirit" (John 3:5, 6).

Doctrine of Revelation

[CS] "The material record of the Bible . . . is no more important to our well being than the history of Europe and America" (*Misc. Writ.*, 170). "The Scriptures cannot properly be interpreted in a literal way. . . . the literal rendering of the Scriptures makes them nothing valuable, but often is the foundation of unbelief and hopelessness" (*Misc. Writ.*, 169).

[RS] "The Science of Mind is not a special revelation of any individual; it is, rather, the culmination of all revelations" (*S/M*, 35).

"REVELATION— . . . Since the mind that man uses is the same Mind that God uses, the One and Only Mind, the avenues of Revelation can never be closed. But no man can receive the Revelation for another" (*S/M*, 630).

[USC] "Scripture may be a satisfactory authority for those who are not themselves in direct communion with the Lord" (*Unity Magazine*, no.7, Oct. 1896, p. 400). "Spiritual principle is embodied in the sacred books of the world's living religions. Christians . . . believe that the Bible is the greatest and most keenly spiritual of all Scriptures, though they realize that other

"Sanctify them by the truth; your word is truth" (John 17:17). [Jesus speaking to the Father.]

"The Scripture cannot be broken" (John 10:35).

"All Scripture is God-breathed and is useful for teaching, rebuking, correcting, and training in righteousness" (2 Tim. 3:16).

"We do not use deception, *nor do we distort the word of God*. On the contrary, *by setting forth the truth plainly* we commend ourselves to every man's conscience in the sight of God" (2 Cor. 4:2).

"Contend for the faith that was *once for all* entrusted to the saints" (Jude 3).

"To the law and to the testimony! If they do not speak according to this word, they have no light of dawn" (Isa. 8:20).

"*Every word* of God is *flawless. . . . Do not add to his words*, or he will rebuke you and prove you a liar" (Prov. 30:5–6; cf. Rev. 22:18–19; Deut. 4:2).

Scriptures such as the *Zend-Avesta* and the *Upanishads*, as well as the teachings of Buddha, the *Koran*, and the *Tao of Lao-tse* and the writings of Confucius, contain expressions of eminent spiritual truths . . ." (*What Unity Teaches*, 4).

Reincarnation Versus Resurrection

[USC] "We believe that the dissolution of spirit, soul, and body, caused by death, is annulled by rebirth of the same spirit and soul in another body here on earth. We believe the repeated incarnations of man to be a merciful provision of our loving Father to the end that all may have opportunity to attain immortality through regeneration, as did Jesus" (*Unity's Statement of Faith*, Art. 22).

[USC] "Reincarnation replaces the old belief in condemnation and damnation by the faith of the everlasting mercy and forgiveness of God. Neither does our heavenly Father condemn or punish His children" (*Reincarnation*, 3).

[USC] "Reincarnation gives to the soul and spirit of man who sins or makes mistakes repeated opportunities, until he learns to live in conformity with God's law. When man learns to live and apply the truth as did Jesus Christ then the necessity for reincarnation will be done away with. He will have learned to live without dying. . . . The goal of man is eternal life, and in each incarnation that goal is brought nearer" (*Reincarnation*, 5, 8).

"Then Christ would have had to suffer many times since the creation of the world. But now he has appeared *once for all* at the end of the ages *to do away with sin by the sacrifice of himself*. Just as man is destined to *die once*, and *after that to face judgment*, so *Christ was sacrificed once to take away the sins of many people*; and he will appear a second time, not to bear sin, but *to bring salvation* to those who are waiting for him" (Heb. 9:26–28).

"We are confident, I say, and would prefer to be *away from the body and at home with the Lord*. For *we must all appear before the judgment seat of Christ*, that each one may receive what is due him for the things done in the body, whether good or bad" (2 Cor. 5:8, 10). [For the believer, to be absent from the body means to be present with the Lord.]

"Then he will say to those on his left, 'Depart from me, you who are cursed, into the eternal fire prepared for the devil and his angels.' Then they will go away to *eternal* punishment, but the righteous to *eternal* life" (Matt. 25:41, 46).